Hawaii's Hidden Treasures

This first edition belongs to

Name Date

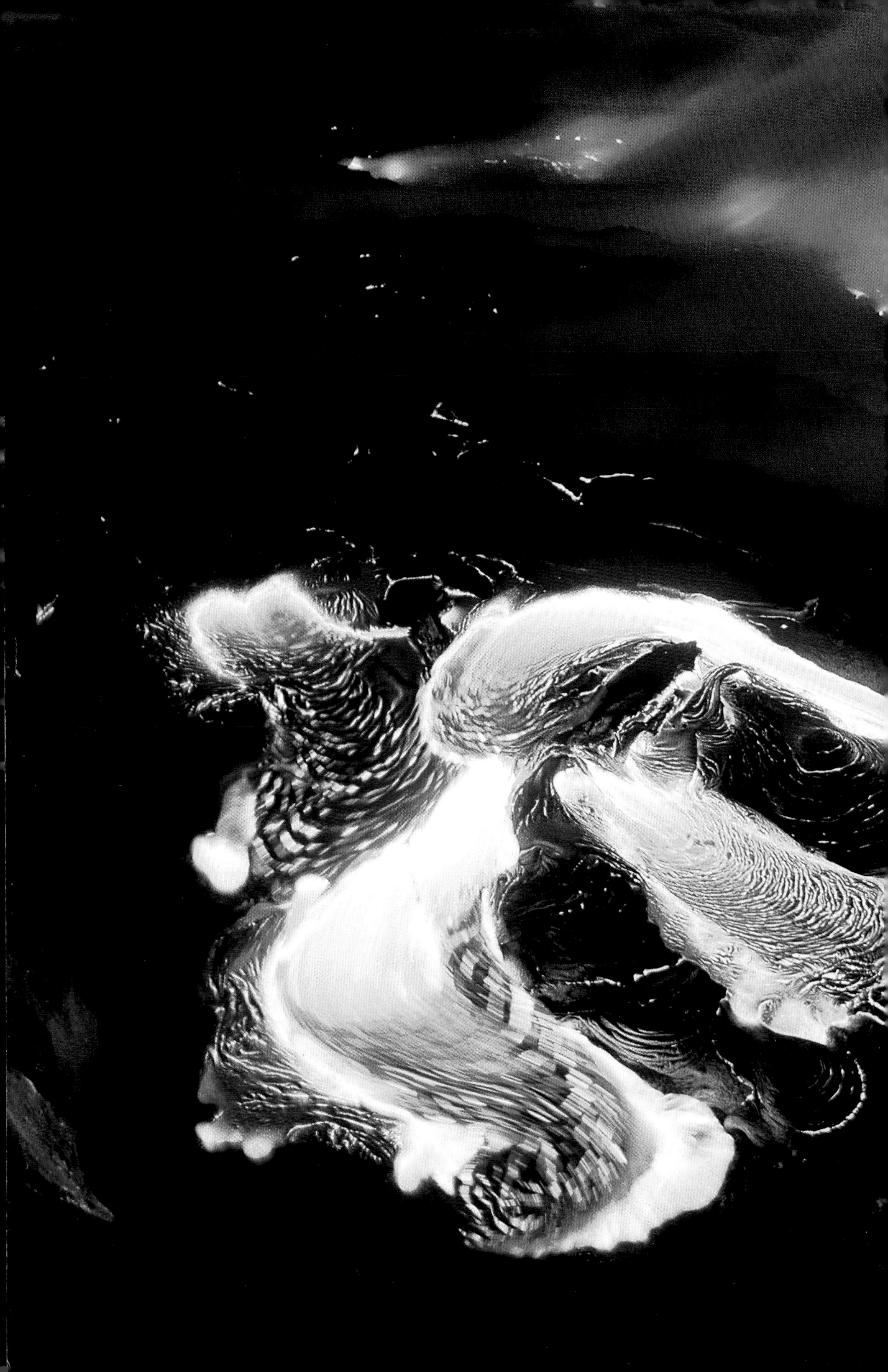

HAWAII'S
HIDDEN TREASURES

BY CYNTHIA RUSS RAMSAY
PHOTOGRAPHED BY CHRIS JOHNS

Prepared by the Book Division
National Geographic Society, Washington, D.C.

Page 1: Clasping a **ho'okupu,** *a dancer makes an offering to the goddess Pele at her traditional lair on Hawaii's Kilauea volcano. Pages 2–3: Incandescent tongues of lava roll toward the sea near Kamoamoa Campground on Hawaii's southeast coast.*

Scuba divers probe a pair of lava tubes extending into the ocean off the island of Hawaii. Such conduits form when the outer surfaces of a lava flow cool, creating a channel for hotter, more liquid rock flowing within.

RICHARD ALEXANDER COOKE III (PAGE 1)

DAVID DOUBILET

HAWAII'S
HIDDEN TREASURES

By Cynthia Russ Ramsay
Photographed by Chris Johns

Published by The National Geographic Society
Gilbert M. Grosvenor,
President and Chairman of the Board
Michela A. English, *Senior Vice President*

Prepared by The Book Division
William R. Gray, *Director*
Margery G. Dunn,
Charles Kogod, *Assistant Directors*

Staff for this Book
Ron Fisher, *Managing Editor*
John G. Agnone, *Illustrations Editor*
Suez B. Kehl, *Art Director*
Victoria Garrett Jones,
Rebecca H. Lescaze, *Researchers*
Melanie Patt-Corner, *Contributing Researcher*
Mary B. Dickinson, *Contributing Editor*
Richard M. Crum, Edward Lanouette,
Cynthia Russ Ramsay,
Jennifer C. Urquhart, *Picture Legend Writers*
Carl Mehler, *Map Editor*
Al Kettler, *Map Art*
Joseph F. Ochlak, Martin S. Walz,
Map Research and Production

Sandra F. Lotterman, *Editorial Assistant*
Karen Dufort Sligh, *Illustrations Assistant*

Lewis R. Bassford, *Production Project Manager*
Timothy H. Ewing, Heather Guwang,
H. Robert Morrison, Richard S. Wain, *Production*
Karen F. Edwards, Elizabeth G. Jevons,
Peggy J. Oxford, Teresita Cóquia Sison,
Marilyn J. Williams, *Staff Assistants*

Manufacturing and Quality Management
George V. White, *Director*
John T. Dunn, *Associate Director*
Vincent P. Ryan, *Manager*
R. Gary Colbert

Bryan K. Knedler, *Indexer*

Library of Congress CIP Data: page 200

Like the spine of a giant sea creature, a furrowed pali*—or cliff—of the Koolau Range draws clouds on windward Oahu, Hawaii's third-largest island. Sun-drenched Honolulu lies in the distance.*

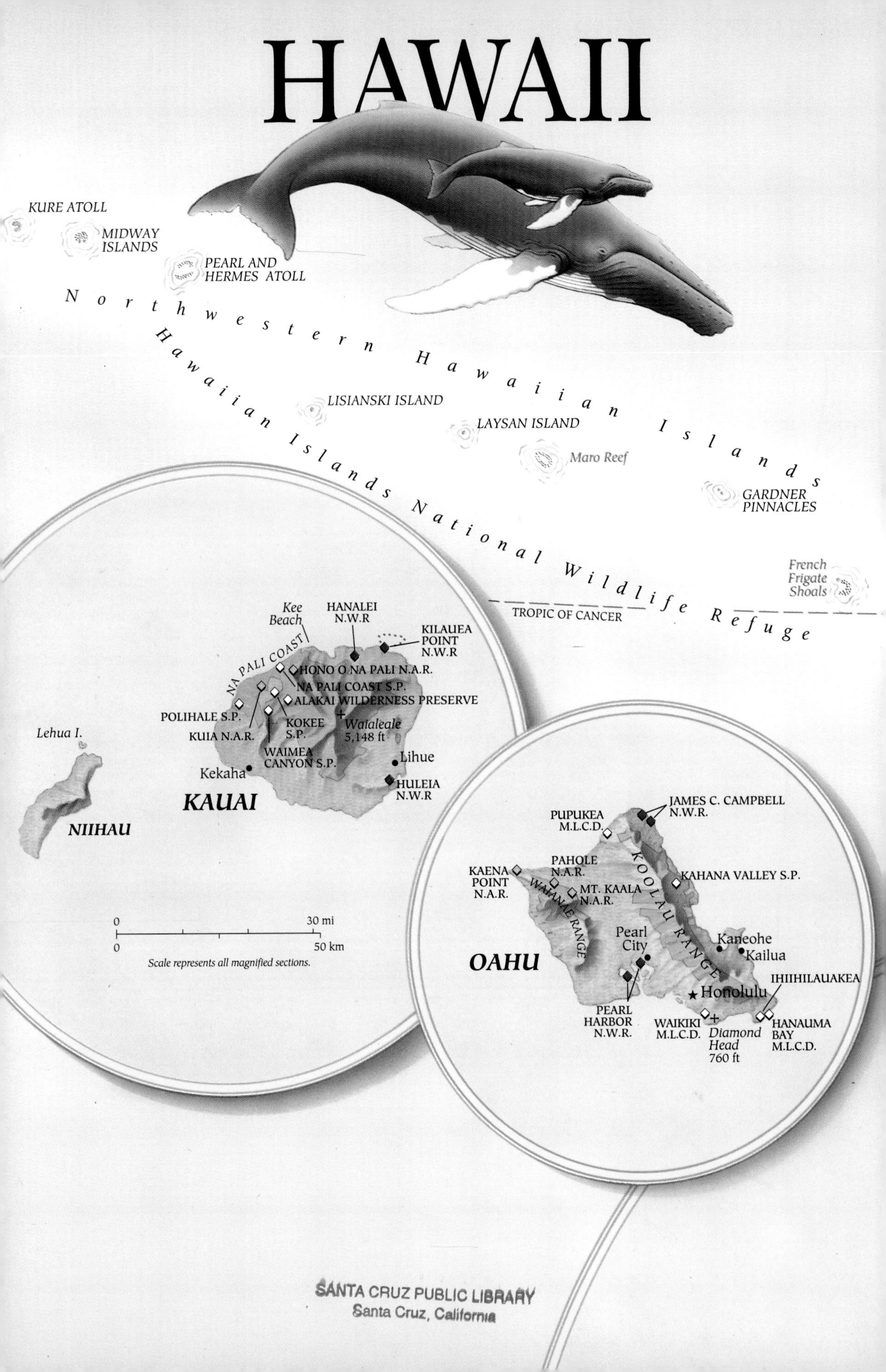
HAWAII
KURE ATOLL
MIDWAY ISLANDS
PEARL AND HERMES ATOLL
Northwestern Hawaiian Islands
Hawaiian Islands National Wildlife Refuge
LISIANSKI ISLAND
LAYSAN ISLAND
Maro Reef
GARDNER PINNACLES
French Frigate Shoals
TROPIC OF CANCER
Kee Beach
HANALEI N.W.R
KILAUEA POINT N.W.R
NA PALI COAST
HONO O NA PALI N.A.R.
NA PALI COAST S.P.
ALAKAI WILDERNESS PRESERVE
POLIHALE S.P.
KUIA N.A.R.
KOKEE S.P.
Waialeale 5,148 ft
WAIMEA CANYON S.P.
Lihue
Kekaha
HULEIA N.W.R
Lehua I.
KAUAI
NIIHAU
0 30 mi
0 50 km
Scale represents all magnified sections.
JAMES C. CAMPBELL N.W.R.
PUPUKEA M.L.C.D.
PAHOLE N.A.R.
KAENA POINT N.A.R.
KOOLAU RANGE
KAHANA VALLEY S.P.
MT. KAALA N.A.R.
WAIANAE RANGE
Pearl City
Kaneohe
Kailua
OAHU
IHIIHILAUAKEA
Honolulu
PEARL HARBOR N.W.R.
WAIKIKI M.L.C.D.
Diamond Head 760 ft
HANAUMA BAY M.L.C.D.

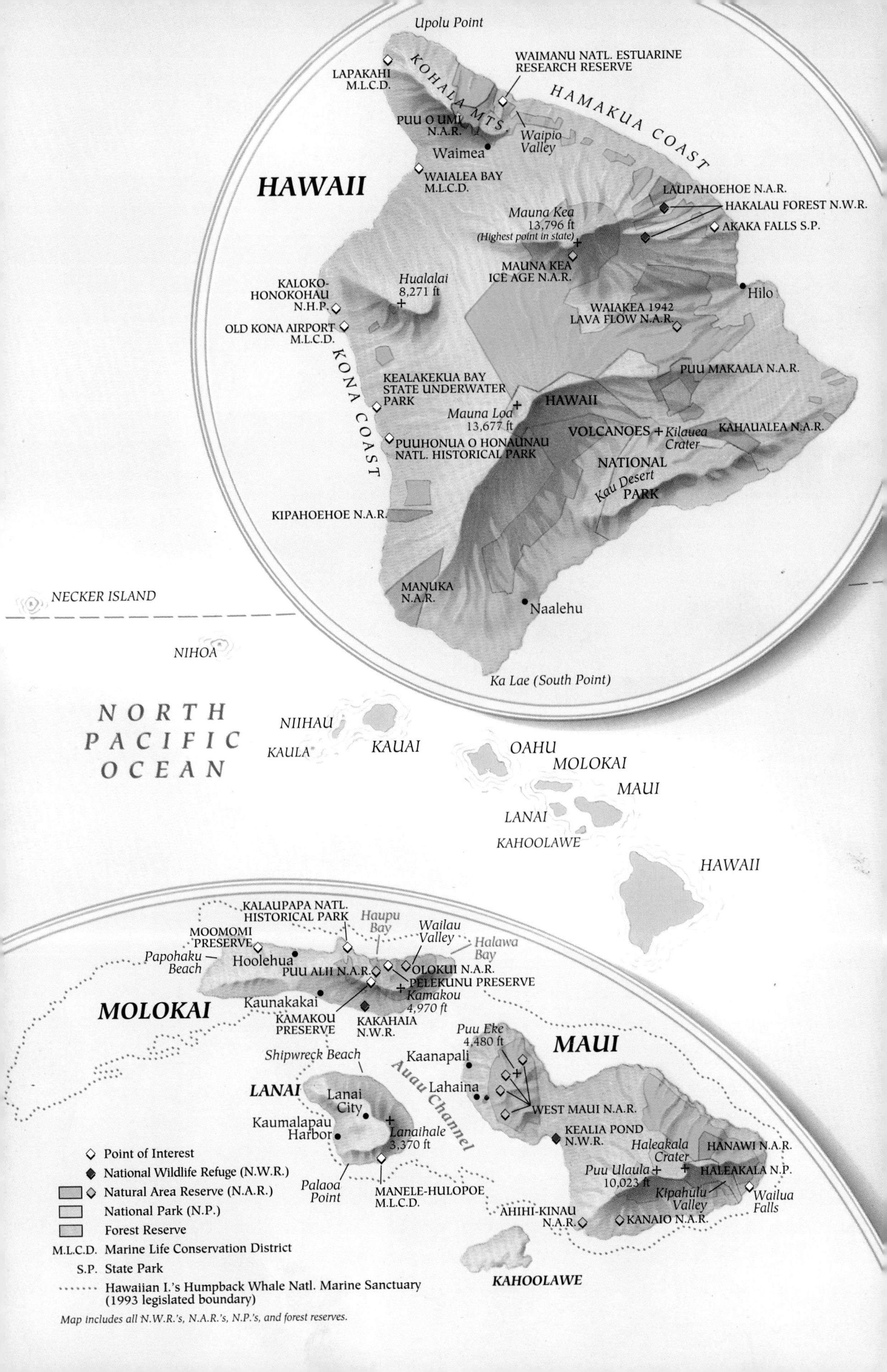

HAWAII
Upolu Point
LAPAKAHI M.L.C.D.
KOHALA MTS.
WAIMANU NATL. ESTUARINE RESEARCH RESERVE
HAMAKUA COAST
PUU O UMI N.A.R.
Waipio Valley
Waimea
WAIALEA BAY M.L.C.D.
LAUPAHOEHOE N.A.R.
HAKALAU FOREST N.W.R.
Mauna Kea 13,796 ft (Highest point in state)
AKAKA FALLS S.P.
MAUNA KEA ICE AGE N.A.R.
Hualalai 8,271 ft
KALOKO-HONOKOHAU N.H.P.
Hilo
WAIAKEA 1942 LAVA FLOW N.A.R.
OLD KONA AIRPORT M.L.C.D.
KONA COAST
PUU MAKAALA N.A.R.
KEALAKEKUA BAY STATE UNDERWATER PARK
HAWAII VOLCANOES NATIONAL PARK
Mauna Loa 13,677 ft
Kilauea Crater
KAHAUALEA N.A.R.
PUUHONUA O HONAUNAU NATL. HISTORICAL PARK
Kau Desert
KIPAHOEHOE N.A.R.
MANUKA N.A.R.
Naalehu
Ka Lae (South Point)
NECKER ISLAND
NIHOA
NORTH PACIFIC OCEAN
NIIHAU
KAULA
KAUAI
OAHU
MOLOKAI
MAUI
LANAI
KAHOOLAWE
HAWAII
KALAUPAPA NATL. HISTORICAL PARK
Haupu Bay
Wailau Valley
Halawa Bay
MOOMOMI PRESERVE
Papohaku Beach
Hoolehua
OLOKUI N.A.R.
PUU ALII N.A.R.
PELEKUNU PRESERVE
Kamakou 4,970 ft
Kaunakakai
MOLOKAI
KAMAKOU PRESERVE
KAKAHAIA N.W.R.
Puu Eke 4,480 ft
MAUI
Shipwreck Beach
Kaanapali
Auau Channel
LANAI
Lanai City
Lahaina
WEST MAUI N.A.R.
Kaumalapau Harbor
Lanaihale 3,370 ft
KEALIA POND N.W.R.
Haleakala Crater
HANAWI N.A.R.
Puu Ulaula 10,023 ft
HALEAKALA N.P.
Palaoa Point
MANELE-HULOPOE M.L.C.D.
Kipahulu Valley
Wailua Falls
AHIHI-KINAU N.A.R.
KANAIO N.A.R.
KAHOOLAWE
Point of Interest
National Wildlife Refuge (N.W.R.)
Natural Area Reserve (N.A.R.)
National Park (N.P.)
Forest Reserve
M.L.C.D. Marine Life Conservation District
S.P. State Park
Hawaiian I.'s Humpback Whale Natl. Marine Sanctuary (1993 legislated boundary)
Map includes all N.W.R.'s, N.A.R.'s, N.P.'s, and forest reserves.

By Hannah Kihalani Springer, Hawaiian

'O au no 'O Hannah Kihalani Springer.
'O au ka pulapula o Kihalani laua me Pilipo.
'O au he kama o ku'u 'aina aloha. 'O Kukui'ohiwai ka inoa.
'O au no he kama'aina.

"I am Hannah Kihalani Springer.
I am the off-shoot of my parents, Kihalani and Pilipo.
I am a child of my beloved homeland. Kukui'ohiwai by name.
I am *kama'aina*, a child of the land."

The above declaration, in Hawaiian and English, is both fact and metaphor. It establishes my relationship with my family and with my home, 2,000 feet up on the northwest flank of Hualalai on the island of Hawaii. Kukui'ohiwai has been my family's home for five, going on six, generations. We live with a view of the place where a set of my seven-times-great-grandparents lie at rest by the sea. I am the only child of a first-born child of an only child of a first-born child of an only child—and we are all female and carry the name Kihalani.

As a lifelong student of Hawaii, I claim the perspective of a *kama'aina*—with an affinity for and an intimacy with my islands. When I learn something new of my homeland, it is like a memory from a cherished elder. As a Hawaiian, I believe that my elders are recalled by voicing certain words and names, by visiting certain places, or by seeing certain life-forms. The sight of a *pueo*—a Hawaiian owl—swooping across the grasslands evokes wonderment in any of us, but I have been taught that this bird is an alternate body form associated with a revered ancestor from the Lahaina area of Maui.

Hawaii is the most isolated archipelago in the world. From where I live, I can see black expanses of lava flows 200 years old that are being slowly colonized by plants. During the eons before my time, the volcanic islands of Hawaii were similarly colonized: A unique mix of plants and animals drifted here from other parts of the globe and evolved into life-forms found nowhere else.

Much of Hawaii's natural environment has been irrevocably altered by development and by tenacious invaders—exotic plants and animals that overwhelm native species. Golf courses, resorts, housing, a cemetery, and a college, all this and more have been proposed near my home. Massive earth-moving equipment is doing in hours what centuries of erosion could not do.

My mother tongue—soft and lilting when spoken, confusingly vowel-rich in print—uses symbols perhaps unfamiliar to many readers of this book: Glottal stops—reverse apostrophes—represent a break in mid-sound in a word; a macron over a letter indicates a long vowel.

Hawaii's Hidden Treasures offers an opportunity for all of us to benefit from kama'aina insight. Many of the people whose lives we touch in this book, people who are working with diligence, sincerity, and aloha for the survival of remnants of Hawaii's unique places, are indeed kama'aina.

You will recognize us. Images here—both in photographs and in words—give insight into the natural and cultural forces that have shaped me and my kin. They are the images of Hawaii. They are a portrait of my family.

Traditional ti leaves comprise a dancer's skirt, but for her wristlets she uses dyed domestic feathers; Hawaii's yellow-feathered birds are now largely extinct.

RICHARD ALEXANDER COOKE III

Shaping the Island

Trees lay charred and smoldering. Clouds of steam exploded into the sky where the river of molten rock poured into the sea. Searing heat billowed out of the fiery stream, which crackled like gunfire as the flow of lava snapped the thin, dark crust that formed on the cooling surface. In daylight these fissures looked like a gleaming web. At night the entire mass was aglow, and the sky reflected the red glare of the burning lava and gas, flooding the darkness with a lurid light.

The architect of these events on the Big Island was Kilauea, the world's most active volcano. A long-lived eruption began on January 3, 1983, as molten rock within the earth, called magma, forced its way some ten miles into the volcano's east rift zone, a system of fractured rock. The tremendous pressures pushed the cracks apart, and lava 2,000°F surged up from these new fissures in curtains of fire that flamed on the land like emblems of divine rage.

In the next phase, countless tons of lava roared out of a single vent every three or four weeks, spurting in golden geysers as high as the Empire State Building. As the lava cooled and congealed into cinders and spatter, it fell like dark rain into the fountain's fiery brightness. This fallout debris gradually built a small mountain, an 835-foot cone named Pu'u 'Ō'ō, after the extinct *'ō'ō* bird.

In July 1986 the eruption moved two miles down the rift zone and formed a lava pond that spewed a nearly constant torrent of molten rock down the mountainside for about four years. Eventually the lava reached the ocean. For much of the way, it flowed through tubes that formed as the surface lava cooled and solidified. These tunnels insulated the lava within, so it remained hot and fluid for long distances. When it emerged on the lush southeast coast, it still burned with a terrible fury.

"No one thought the lava would travel seven miles to the sea," said Harry Kim, the island's civil defense administrator, speaking in his office in Hilo, the island's county seat. He had been in charge of evacuating residents from several seaside hamlets and subdivisions in the lava's path.

Harry tried to give people as much time as possible to take a last look at their land and homes. "People knew they would be leaving their community forever," he explained. "After a flood you can return and clean up. You can also rebuild after a fire. But there was no going back after the lava rolled over Kalapana. The landmarks were buried. Even the contours of the land had changed. Nothing is recognizable except the horizon."

I walked on top of Kalapana—on top of the store, church, and 100 homes entombed 25 to 100 feet below the expanse of glossy black lava, cool now but still contoured with the swirls and ripples of its flow. This lava

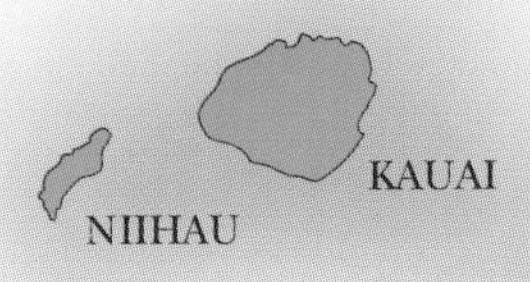

CHAIN

was of a smooth, fluid variety known as pahoehoe. The other form, called a'a, is rough and chunky and looks like rubble. Beneath the pahoehoe were gardens once bountiful with bananas and papayas, graveyards people had tended with loving care, and an idyllic, palm-fringed arc of black sand called Kaimū Beach. My stroll also took me to the newest land on earth, for the eruptions had extended the shoreline almost a quarter of a mile into the sea and created 300 acres of new land where nothing but ocean had existed before.

The trade winds were blowing hard, rushing clouds across the sky and ruffling the ocean with short, pointed waves. Heavy surf foamed against a spur of low, black cliffs—a scene made more eloquent by a rainbow shimmering in the spray. But nothing stirred on the lifeless ground. The petrified landscape, utterly empty, was so full of silence it magnified the boom of the sea on the rocky shore.

The prolonged eruption evicted hundreds of Hawaiians from their homes but never threatened lives. Only twice in recorded history has Kilauea been racked by violent explosions. Volcanoes in these islands normally don't blow their tops. Compared to Mount St. Helens, for instance, Hawaiian volcanoes are tame.

From scientists at the Hawaiian Volcano Observatory, an arm of the U.S. Geological Survey on the rim of Kilauea's caldera, I learned why. Hawaiian lava has very little carbon dioxide and water: When these are dissolved in molten rock, they build up tremendous pressures and eventually explode. In addition, Hawaiian lavas are usually hot and fluid, so any gas bubbles that do form can escape harmlessly into the atmosphere.

Scientists at the observatory monitor the mountain like an intensive-care patient. They listen with seismic sensors that record and pinpoint the movement of magma at depths of 30 miles within the earth's mantle. They measure bulges on the volcano's flanks with a tiltmeter, a device so sensitive it could detect the angle made by lifting a mile-long board at one end a mere quarter-inch. A warp on the earth's surface alerts geologists to increased magma pressure underground.

"We've learned a lot about how magma travels through Kilauea's plumbing system. We know there is a reservoir below the summit that feeds the eruptions. We know how much magma is stored there and how it

FOLLOWING PAGES: Curled like a comber, a wall of molten rock meets the sea in an explosive roar along Hawaii's south coast. Spilling from a vent on the slopes of Kilauea, the flow reached temperatures of about 2,000°F.

MAP PRODUCTION BY ALEX TAIT / EQUATOR GRAPHICS

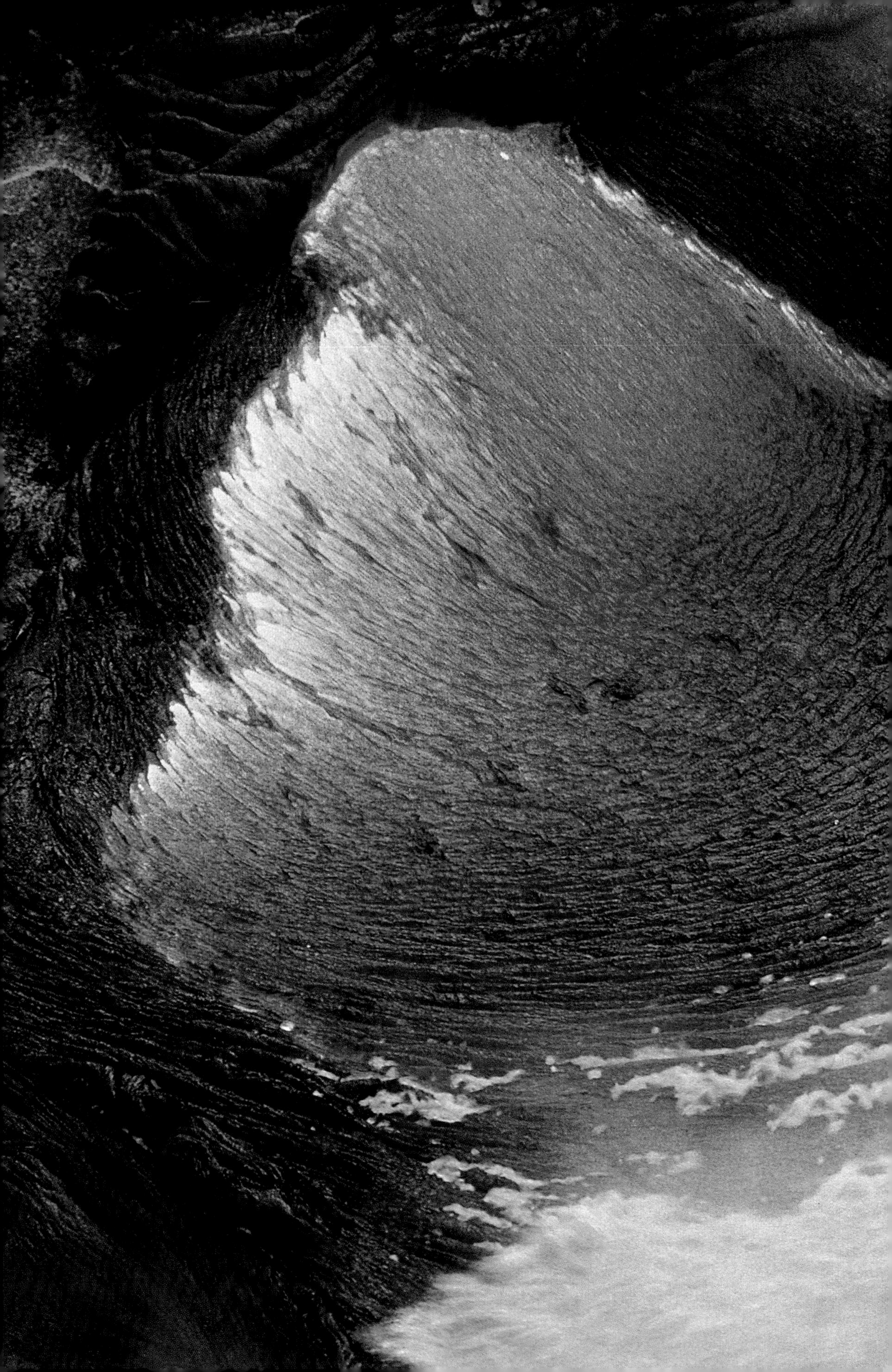

moves," said the observatory's scientist-in-charge, David A. Clague. "Once the volcano goes off, we take samples of the lava to determine its temperature and chemical composition. Changes give us clues to what's happening down inside the storage chamber."

A helicopter was ferrying geologists to the remote eruption site. It had returned to the Pu'u 'O'ō cone, and there was room on board for me to go along. We flew over old lava flows that cut a black swath through a forest. Bleached skeletons of trees stood like specters on the bands of darkness. As we approached the advancing tide of lava, I could see small plumes of steam hovering above the ground like fallen clouds. Then the pilot circled briefly over the crater where a small lava pond seethed just below the rim, radiant with the blaze of liquid rock.

"Molten metal has not that crimson gleam, nor blood that living light," wrote Scottish author Isabella L. Bird. She described the "glory" and "terror" of a lava lake on Kilauea in 1873 in her book, *Six Months Among the Palm Groves, Coral Reefs and Volcanoes of the Sandwich Islands,* as Westerners called Hawaii in the 19th century.

We landed at the base of the cone, a few hundred feet from where the lava was oozing downhill. It was emerging from a vent that had burst through the cone's flanks. While geologists scooped up gobs of hot, moving lava with a special shovel and made calculations to determine the volume of the flow, I plodded up the loose cinder slope.

Black fumes poured from the vent, which roared like a hundred blowtorches. The heat, merely uncomfortable at first, became a brutal onslaught as I advanced uphill. The noise, the intense heat, the sulfur smell, and the river burning like no earthly thing assaulted my mind as well as my senses. This was liquid rock bleeding from our planet's molten heart. I was standing before the planetary power that had built all the islands, witness to one of nature's grandest spectacles.

Like Isabella Bird, I felt removed and "altogether out of the range of ordinary life," for I had a front-row seat at a drama that has been playing in the Pacific Ocean for 70 million years. I also felt the same little shock of recognition, realizing how utterly volcanic the islands are. Very nearly "every stone, atom of dust, and foot of fruitful or barren soil" is of this igneous origin.

Lava flowing layer upon layer for eons has raised more than a hundred volcanoes from the seafloor, creating an immense mountain range that stands mostly underwater and stretches some 3,600 miles across the Pacific toward Alaska's Aleutian Islands. The Hawaiian archipelago lies at the southeastern end of this long volcanic chain. These mountains, the tallest and most isolated in the world, break the surface of the sea at about 18,000 feet, and the main Hawaiian islands are the summits of these mighty peaks. To the northwest of Kauai, the mountains have been worn away, reduced to about a hundred islets, rock pinnacles, and coral reefs.

These low-lying scraps of land strewn across 1,091 miles of ocean constitute the Northwestern Hawaiian Islands, or Leewards, a virtually uninhabited, little-known part of the state.

North of the Hawaiian archipelago, all the volcanoes are completely lost from view. They form a submarine range—the Emperor Seamounts. "Core and dredge samples show that these drowned mountains were made of the same kinds of lava and were built up from the ocean floor in the same way as the Hawaiian islands," said David, back at the observatory.

Most of the world's volcanoes occur in the zones of weakness, where giant, slow-moving tectonic plates—segments of the earth's crust—rub and collide as they drift like icebergs atop the mantle. But the Hawaiian-Emperor volcanoes are exceptions; they are the products of a hot spot at least 60 to 90 miles down in the interior of the earth.

A hot spot is a place where molten rock is generated on a very large scale. Most geologists agree that its source is a huge, upwelling column, or "plume," of mantle rock ascending through the mantle; it rises because it is hotter than the surrounding rock, or chemically different, or both. When the temperature is high enough or the pressure has been reduced enough as the plume ascends, the rock partially melts and pushes through the earth's crust, triggering volcanic activity on the surface.

This mysterious wellspring of lava is stationary while the Pacific plate drifts over it, moving northwestward about four inches a year. As if on an assembly line, the hot spot spawns volcanoes in succession, and like a conveyor belt the ocean plate trundles them off toward the Aleutian Trench, where the seafloor bends into the earth's interior. Riding the Pacific plate is a slow way to travel, for the seamount farthest from the hot spot began its journey 70 million years ago.

Scientists estimate that Kauai, the oldest of the eight main Hawaiian islands, rose above the waves about five or six million years ago. The terrain is progressively younger moving down the chain from Niihau to Oahu, Molokai, Lanai, uninhabited Kahoolawe, and Maui, where the principal lava flows are only about a million years old. Hawaii, the youngest island—also known as the Big Island—is still growing. But the trail of lava actually continues some 20 miles southeast of the Big Island to the Loihi Seamount, still 3,000 feet below the ocean surface.

In tens of thousands of years, Loihi probably will be a small island rising above Hawaii's deep blue waters, bursting forth in great tempests of steam. In less than a million years this heap of lava could grow into a great dome so high its summit would be besieged by snow and frost. With the passage of time, when rains, rivers, and the ocean gnaw away the lava, and gravity assails the stone, Loihi will be worn down to small rock pinnacles and then, like the Emperor Seamounts, disappear beneath the waves.

The ancient Hawaiians recognized the signs of age in the landforms and enshrined the chronology of the islands in their myths. According to one legend, the islands were pulled up out of the sea with a magic fishhook by the demigod and culture hero Maui. The sequence matches the actual volcanic history of the chain.

Pele, the ancient Hawaiians' "goddess of the burning stones," is responsible for eruptions. She travels down the island chain forging volcanic craters and cinder cones in a quest for a home. Again and again her efforts are defeated by a sea goddess who *(Continued on page 24)*

Pu'u 'O'ō vent, named for an extinct black-and-yellow bird whose feathers once decorated royal capes and helmets, smokes on Kilauea's slopes. The 835-foot-high cone has been the site of spectacular pyrotechnic displays for more than a decade, initially spewing lava fountains up to a thousand feet into the air. Ropy pahoehoe lava (opposite) forms twists and coils on the surface.

FOLLOWING PAGES: A lava river cuts a burning swath through a forest on Kilauea's flanks. The most recent cycle of eruptions, from a vent on the mountain's east flank, began in January 1983.

Volcano at work: Floods of lava gushing down Kilauea's slopes have inundated a village and invaded a subdivision as the molten rock moves toward the sea. In its most recent outbursts, lava first reached the ocean in November 1986 and has since added 300 acres of new land to Hawaii. A solitary fern (opposite) struggles for a toehold amid the desolation of a decade-old flow along a saddle road that runs between the island's two largest volcanoes—Mauna Loa and Mauna Kea.

quenches her flames. Each time Pele flees farther south in the chain, taking a route that very nearly follows the geologic age of the islands. At Kilauea she finds a permanent home in a large crater in the floor of the summit caldera. Called Halemaumau, it seethed with lava for most of the years between 1823 and 1924.

Today the lava lake has drained underground and the floor of the crater is covered by a 1974 flow. But its fires have merely been banked, for tendrils of vapor and sulfurous gases boil out of vents in Halemaumau's congealed surface and drift like incense over the goddess's desolate domain.

Kilauea still lures visitors to Hawaii Volcanoes National Park, where they hope to see the volcano in action. But the park is also a showcase of a variety of volcanic landscapes. Lavas of different ages create a tapestry ranging from the stony expanses where life first takes hold to old forests of gnarly ohia trees with ferns at their feet. There are long stretches of craggy, stone-banked shores, where beach morning glories leave a trail of lavender blossoms on small crescents of sand. In the Kau Desert, solitary sprigs curl out of clefts in the rock, and large white-tailed tropic birds, back from feeding in the sea, swoop and soar above their nests, their long tail streamers arcing above that large emptiness.

Kilauea's elevation is a scant 4,090 feet. Pele has another, much larger abode on the Big Island—the Mauna Loa volcano, a next-door neighbor. Mauna Loa last went off in 1984, spewing a colossal million cubic yards of lava an hour for three weeks—enough to fill about two million railroad cars. Mauna Loa reaches a height of 13,677 feet, but measured from the ocean floor it is taller than Mount Everest. In sheer mass, Mauna Loa is the largest mountain on the planet.

Seen from a distance, it looks deceptively low, merely an elongated hill against the sky. Highly fluid lava flows have produced the broad summit and gentle slopes of a shield volcano. Isabella Bird called it "an unfinished mountain." Indeed, Mauna Loa has no rivers or even permanent streams to dissect its contours into valleys and glens.

As University of Hawaii geologist George P. L. Walker explained: "The lava is highly porous. Gas bubbles have left many spaces—vesicles—in the rock, so even in a heavy rain, water just sinks into the ground instead of running off into streams. Later in a shield volcano's life cycle, when eruptions become less frequent, weathering takes place and the lava is covered with less permeable soil. That's when you start getting valley erosion."

For a hint of things next in store for Kilauea and Mauna Loa, I had only to look at the three other volcanoes that have built the island of Hawaii—Hualalai, Mauna Kea, and Kohala. All five together have given the island almost two-thirds of the land area of the entire state.

Hualalai, rising steeply over the Kona coast on the island's western

Blown by wind and washed by water, a hibiscus blossom brightens a beach along Hawaii's north coast. Some 1,800 plant species grow in the Hawaiian chain; 90 percent of the 1,100 native species are unique to the islands.

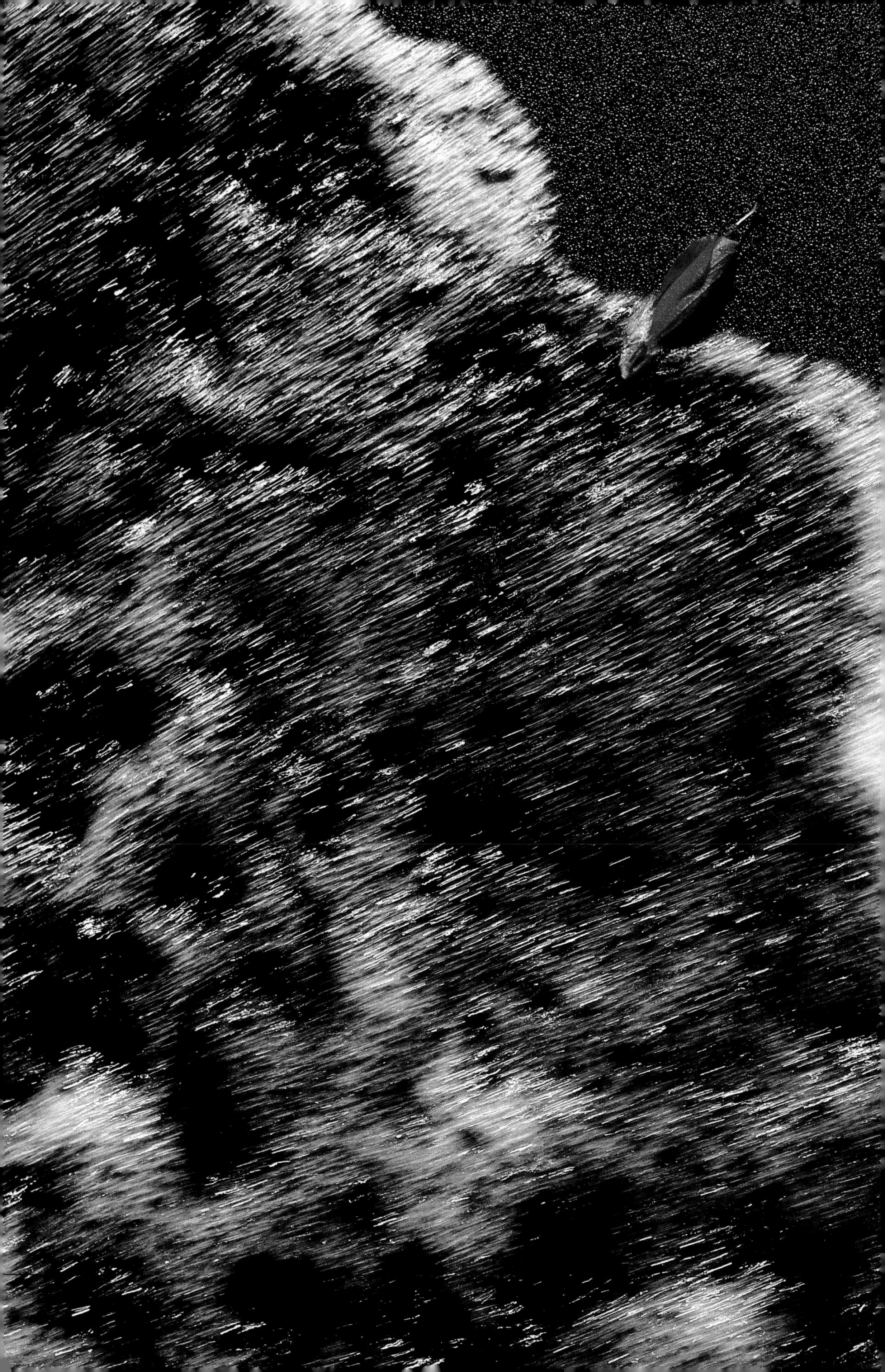

shores, may be past the prime of life, but for the last thousand years it has erupted an average of once every two centuries. The last eruption was in 1801, and geologists think another could occur in the next century. They consider the volcano to be the most dangerous on the island because its lava flows very fast. "Last time it reached the coast in a matter of hours," said Hannah Kihalani Springer, a young woman whose Polynesian ancestors lived on land in the path of the lava.

It was only late morning, yet we had no view of Hualalai, for it was already swaddled in clouds that formed as mountain updrafts sucked moisture from the sea. Although the Kona coast is on the drier, leeward side of the island, Mauna Loa, Mauna Kea, and Hualalai are such large, tall masses that they absorb enough heat to generate local air currents that draw moisture from the ocean. By afternoon the air is saturated, and, quite predictably, by three or four o'clock it rains in the uplands.

Yet Hawaiians called a part of this district *kekaha wai 'ole*—land without water—because the north slope of youthful Hualalai is like a sponge, and what rain falls there drains quickly underground.

In the past, the rains sustained groves of breadfruit and gardens planted with sweet potatoes, bananas, gourds, sugarcane, and dryland taro, but for drinking water the people used lava tubes as walk-in wells. "They would go down into the tunnels to collect water dripping from the rock above," Hannah said.

The summit of Hualalai provides grand vistas of Mauna Kea, slightly higher than Mauna Loa, and at 13,796 feet the highest island mountain in the world. In some winters snow mantles the volcano, transforming Mauna Kea into a dazzling white prominence in the tropical sky. In 1983, standing on the summit of Hualalai, Hannah witnessed a spectacle on Mauna Kea and Mauna Loa of another sort. An earthquake shook the island so violently that boulders and rocks tumbled into the hundreds of cinder cones on their flanks. Great plumes of dust spouted from all those craters, rising into the sky like smoke from a city under siege.

Cinder cones are the first signs of age for Hawaii's volcanoes. The late-stage eruptions that produced these cones were a longtime mystery. Scientists wondered what triggered them if the island-volcano had drifted past the hot spot. Revised theories provide an answer. Until recently, the hot spot was depicted as a pipeline conduit, but geologists now believe that when the mantle plume strikes the lithosphere—the rigid outer part of the earth—it spreads into a broad mushroom shape. Thus, the hot spot is several hundred miles wide. It is hotter in the center but retains enough heat in the outer zones to produce these later sporadic explosive eruptions.

In this phase the chemical composition of the magma changes and has a higher gas content, so it doesn't flow to the surface. Instead, it rockets into the air in fragments that cool and shatter as they fall, piling up in large cinder cones around the vents.

Mauna Kea also shows signs of age in the V-shaped gulches on its eastern flanks, where streams have begun to sluice away the stone. At this gully erosion stage, running water has cut deep clefts in the hillsides.

Author Isabella Bird counted 69 of these verdant chasms within a distance of 30 miles along the shores north of Hilo. The waterfalls are too many and some are too ephemeral for a definite count, but even in a drought year I saw more than a dozen, shining like tinsel amid the dark, jungly profusion of the ravines. In one sheer drop, 'Akaka Falls plummets 442 feet, lavishing mist and enchantment on a forest ornamented with pink and red bougainvillea and red torches of ginger.

How different it was on the Waimea Plains, a high tableland at 2,500 feet. The clouds had dissipated, and grasses blanketed the undulating countryside, where cattle grazed pasturelands that might have been in the American West. In the lee of Mauna Kea, the land receives much less rainfall than the windward coast. Watercourses leave only shallow imprints, and Mauna Kea's cinder cones retain sharp profiles under a thin mantle of grass.

Almost everywhere in the islands the weather is influenced by the trade winds, which blow from the northeast and pass over thousands of miles of ocean before they collide with the high peaks. The slopes force this damp air up into the cooler heights, where the moisture condenses until the clouds are heavy enough to deliver rain. By the time the air reaches the leeward coasts, it has been wrung dry, and rainfall is down to ten inches a year. Traveling west on Highway 19, past Waimea to the Kohola coast, I could trace the decline. Grasses gradually faded and dwindled to a sparse growth that in the late afternoon light tinged the dark lava land with gold.

North, beyond the plains at Mauna Kea's feet, the terrain owes its origin to Kohala, a volcano that hissed and steamed to the surface some 700,000 years ago. Since then, an eye blink in geologic time, the mountain lost its roundness, and 12 miles of its windward coast gained deep valleys and audacious cliffs that rise from the sea on pedestals of foam.

Not all the landscapes that take one's breath away were shaped by rain, rivers, and waves that undercut the stone. Recent discoveries indicate that the cliffs of Kohala were created by a massive landslide that wrenched several miles off the coast.

It was only a few years ago that geologists learned just how unstable Hawaii's mountains are. No one had realized how much of the islands have slumped to the bottom of the sea. Monumental landslides sheared off parts of Molokai and Kauai and were the genesis of their spectacular coastlines. In the last few years, ship-towed sonar has produced images of the ocean floor around all the islands that clearly show vast hummocks of rubble that match the rock on shore.

Oahu's Koolau Range is another stunning product of these cataclysmic avalanches. To see the mountains from a geologist's perspective, I drove up the Pali Highway with Professor Walker. We stopped at the Nuuanu turnout for a view of the cliffs with their lovely vertical lines.

"You are looking at little more than half of what was once a shield volcano," said George. "The other half collapsed and fell away into the ocean about two million years ago.The collapse was a single catastrophic event of a magnitude that has not occurred in recorded history. The sea waves produced by these debris avalanches were so immense they would wash away every building we have in Hawaii today."

Punctuated by red blossoms of African tulip trees, lush rain forest

According to some geologists, there is evidence for such a mammoth tsunami on the island of Lanai. Limestone deposits on a hillside of black lava strongly suggest that gigantic waves swept the remains of a coral reef up to an elevation of a thousand feet.

To help explain why Hawaii's volcanoes collapse, George took me to a nearby quarry that exposes about 500 vertical bands of dark rock side by side. "This is literally the heart of the Koolau volcano. It is what Kilauea looks like below the surface. Each band represents an eruption that injected magma into a crack and solidified underground. These intrusions, called dikes, created pressures that eventually pried the mountain apart."

Long after lava flows had built the Koolau shield and long after half the mountain slid into the sea, the tranquil volcano sprang back to life in a phenomenon geologists call rejuvenated, or post-erosional, volcanism.

DOUGLAS PEEBLES

greenery blankets a windward slope of Mauna Kea.

After the volcano had played dead for a million years, a flurry of activity rocked the Koolau Range and produced a cluster of cones on the southeastern end of the island. In some cases lava struck water-saturated rock and flashed into steam. These were fiendish blasts that pulverized lava and launched clouds of ash into the sky. When the debris fell, it formed broad cones that solidified into a substance called tuff.

One of these cones, formed in one enormous explosion, has become a Honolulu landmark called Diamond Head. In the early 1800s British sailors hiking its slopes mistook calcite crystals for diamonds, and the error gave the tuff crater its name. I saw its famed silhouette rising grandly from the sea near Waikiki Beach on my first evening in the islands. The western sky was pink, and the sands of the broad beach gleamed like alabaster. A breeze brought a rustle to the palms, a sound as mellow as the lazy splash of the surf along the shore. Despite the rampart of hotels along the beach, Diamond Head was a dramatic presence, a reminder of the volcanic intricacies of the islands.

While landslides, running water, and waves sculpture and cut away the land, the islands are also slowly subsiding as the volcanic crust cools and shrinks. The Big Island, the largest and heaviest of the islands, is sinking fastest. Tide gauge records at Hilo show that from 1946 to 1983 the city was subsiding 4.8 millimeters a year. On Oahu a series of stream-cut valleys have been drowned, endowing the island with deep inlets that provide America's Pacific Fleet with the fine anchorages of Pearl Harbor.

Sea levels also have been restless, fluctuating with the thaws and freezes of ice age glaciers and continental ice sheets. This ebb and flow has given the coral reefs that fringe the main islands a precarious existence.

Corals are tiny, fastidious creatures, requiring clear, warm, sunlit shallows. Living in colonies of billions, they secrete limestone casings for their small selves. When they die, their outer skeletons accumulate as part of a structure on which only the veneer is alive. Many Hawaiian reefs have been swamped by a combination of sinking islands and rising seas. When the corals of the top, living layer could not grow upward into the sunlit zone fast enough, they perished. Other times calamity struck when waters receded and exposed the polyps to the air. On such a coral structure, once the residence of bright-hued fishes, sponges, and sea urchins, most of the city of Honolulu now stands.

On the other hand, in the northwest islands at Kure Atoll, the coral polyps kept pace with the subsidence. They continued to grow toward the surface, building a limestone wreath around the island core even after it had disappeared from view. In places, scraps of broken coral, other debris, and seeds collected on top of these vast reefs, forming islets and sandbars where green turtles, monk seals, and millions of seabirds come to breed. But of the island, with its high peak wreathed in clouds and its cliffs shining with waterfalls, nothing remains. In ten million years its saga had ended.

The Hawaiian islands have another epic story to tell, for they are marvelously unique, inhabited by plants and animals that are found nowhere else in the world. These endemic species include ferns that look like four-leaf clovers, daisies that have evolved into shrubs, and mountaintop bogs with elfin trees. Some of the creatures dwelling in Hawaii are among the oddest on earth. There are shrimps that have adapted to life on land, spiders that impale their prey with spikes on their hind legs, and fish that climb thousands of feet up rushing streams and waterfalls by clinging to rocks with fins like suction cups.

The story of life on these islands began with sterile volcanic rock more than 2,000 miles from the nearest landmass. In the beginning, the lava stood barren, slowly weathering and crumbling into soil. Strictly by chance, life found its way to these strange new landscapes and colonized them, against difficult odds. It arrived, carried on the winds, rafted on flotsam from Asia and the Americas, and washed ashore by the currents. Or it hitched a ride with birds, in their feathers, stomachs, or the mud on their feet.

But there were a multitude of dead ends before life took hold. Seeds did not always germinate. Isolated insects and birds could not mate, and few animals were egg-carrying, fertilized females. For each stray that was able to reproduce, thousands landed and did not multiply. One botanist estimated that an average of one flowering plant took root every twenty to thirty thousand years, a rate that would account for the native species that exist today.

No reptiles arrived, and of land mammals only one species managed to cross the ocean—the Hawaiian hoary bat, a solitary creature that spends the day hanging from a tree. It was a haphazard array of plants and animals that established themselves on the islands. But in the tremendously varied climate and terrain of Hawaii, many pioneers found new niches to exploit and new incentives to diversify. Competitors were at a minimum, and predators, if any, were few, so genetic changes survived that in other places would have been selected out. The islands were a natural laboratory where evolution could experiment, trying this and that.

"In these small, isolated populations, genetic variations, or mutations, did not get averaged out. New characteristics were established quickly, and in time this 'founder effect' produced new species," said Professor Kenneth Y. Kaneshiro. Director of the Hawaiian Evolutionary Biology Program at the University of Hawaii, Ken has been studying the courtship and mating behavior of pomace flies and bases his theories on this work.

"We've learned that sexual selection plays a much more important role in the evolutionary process than biologists have realized," said Ken. "In large populations, it's the choosy females—those who mate with the best males—that keep the species line pure. But when the population is small, as in the early stages of colonization, a very selective female may never come across a male that meets her courtship requirements. So the next generation is produced by indiscriminate females who are satisfied with a less than perfect performance of a genetically determined mating behavior. For a few generations, selective forces favor the loose females. This process rapidly changes the gene pool and may give rise to new genetic combinations better adapted to the new habitat.

"Scientists have applied this model to other insect groups, as well as to vertebrates such as birds, pocket gophers, and mole rats, and it looks like it may have general applications."

Whatever governs the rules of genetic change, the island flora and fauna took their own peculiar paths to the present. A single finchlike ancestor gave rise to 56 species of honeycreepers. From a common tarweed from California have come small shrubs, climbing vines, and 25-foot trees. More than 800 varieties of land snails evolved from an estimated two dozen different progenitor species.

Everywhere I went in the wild corners of Hawaii, I found that the biology was as astonishing as the beauty. The landscapes have value beyond the enchantment of a waterfall or the surreal drama of an expanse of slick rock with bits of green life taking hold. Exploring these islands intrigues the mind and stirs the imagination, for nature in Hawaii is at her most inventive and extravagant best.

Eyes in the sky, Mauna Kea's observatories cluster nearly 14,000 feet above sea level near the summit of Hawaii's highest volcano. Within the domes, nine telescopes—some so light sensitive they could spot a bulb burning on the moon—probe the universe's far reaches. Unpolluted air and more than 300 clear, cloudless nights a year make Mauna Kea an astronomer's paradise. Below, tree ferns, tall Acacia koas, and an ohia tree loom through the mist of a tropical rain forest along a stretch of the Big Island's Saddle Road.

RICHARD ALEXANDER COOKE III

Wai'ilikahi Falls plummets 320 feet into verdant Waimanu Valley, a water-carved gorge along the Big Island's northern coast. The valley, now part of a natural estuarine reserve, once supported a thriving community

of native Hawaiians, who cultivated taro, breadfruit, and bananas.
FOLLOWING PAGES: Whale-Skate Island, the eroded remnant of a volcano, now barely breaks the waves as a low-lying, coral-fringed atoll.

BILL CURTSINGER

Islands of Life

Entomologist Francis G. Howarth was surprised when he came upon some insects while exploring a lava-tube cave on the slopes of Mauna Loa. At first he thought the creatures were simply strays that had wandered into the tunnel. In fact, they were species new to science, and studies begun on that day in 1971 revealed a whole new world of life flourishing inside Hawaiian caves.

Small, pale insects with tiny eyes that do not see and wings that cannot fly inhabit the humid darkness. Blind wolf spiders lurk in the passageways, listening with secret sonar for vibrations produced by a cricket scurrying along the ceiling or a moth fluttering its wings. These sightless predators stalk by feel—and seldom miss. Eyeless planthoppers hear beckoning love songs with sensors on their feet and follow those signals to rendezvous with mates in the dark.

Each cave is a self-contained biological system inhabited by creatures found nowhere else. No two caves are alike, for the species vary from place to place. But in each case, plant roots that grow down through the ceiling are the primary food source that sustains these lightless habitats.

"At first it was hard to believe any life could populate Hawaiian caves," said Frank, in his office in Honolulu's Bishop Museum, the State Museum of Natural and Cultural History. "Hawaiian lava tubes are geologically so young that we assumed there hadn't been enough time to nurture new species with adaptations for living underground permanently. But we're learning that one should assume nothing in evolutionary biology."

In fact, the highly specialized tenants of Hawaiian caves descend from close kin living aboveground. This startling discovery has revised scientific thinking on the pace of evolution, for it shows that species can change much faster than anyone thought. Frank estimates that it took less than 100,000 years for the Big Island's pale cave crickets to develop differences from their dark cousins dwelling on fresh lava fields.

It is hard to imagine a more sterile place than an expanse of new lava. No leaf casts a shadow; no lichens trace a pattern. But it isn't totally barren if you know where to look. The trade winds are always dispersing insects, seeds, and dust in the air. This jetsam, or aeolian litter, drifts into rock crevices or collects in lee corners of the lava's irregular surface.

"This wind-borne larder rings the dinner bell for crickets, and they move up to the table within a month after the lava cools. Wolf spiders, also looking for a meal, follow their prey onto the newborn rock," said Frank.

Ages ago, ancestors of the wolf spider and the cricket ventured underground. Now their blind descendants can't live anywhere else.

Frank's muted voice takes on more power as he makes a plea for

protecting Hawaii's caves. "Once the animals are gone, they are irreplaceable. We cannot ask them to reinvent themselves. The loss of these amazing life-forms would be tragic, for these small, isolated populations are helping us come to a fuller understanding of ecology and evolution."

Lava tubes are small oases of existence—like the kipukas on the slopes of Mauna Loa and Kilauea.

The dictionary defines a kipuka as an area of older terrain surrounded by more recent lava flows. Time after time, forests that took centuries to grow were buried beneath rivers of lava. But sometimes the flow parted and swept around a patch of land, and one acre—or a thousand—escaped devastation, preserving the lushness of a bygone time.

Other small bastions stand out amid the rich mosaic of landscapes on the Big Island. Though not technically kipukas, they also sustain small, isolated communities: the small tract in the Hakalau Forest National Wildlife Refuge with the highest concentration of endangered birds in the state; the summit of Mauna Kea, where most scientists once doubted life could exist; and the deep and beautiful Waipi'o Valley, where the aura of the Hawaiian past lingers like the mist drifting above the taro patches.

Several kipukas on the slopes of Mauna Loa have attracted scientists. One, dubbed Kipuka 9 by biologists, is a walk of less than half a mile from the Saddle Road, a 60-mile route between the two great volcanoes, Mauna Loa and Mauna Kea. An eruption in 1855 encircled a forest some 3,000 years old. It loomed ahead in verdant, primeval splendor above the austere, younger ground.

I took my time on the walk to the kipuka, stopping to look at the pioneer plants that had found nourishment on barren rock. They were Hawaiian breeds, and I would not find them anyplace else.

Sadleria ferns sprouted in clusters, their fronds stiff and leathery to the touch. The scrubby *pūkiawe,* twiggy and prickly with small, narrow leaves, was studded with pink, unpalatable berries. Far sweeter and juicier were the red berries of the *'ōhelo,* a plant of the heath family. They were once considered a favorite of the goddess Pele, and she was said to punish anyone eating them without first offering a portion to her.

Ohia trees, stunted and gnarled, had taken up residence on the rock. Ohias are at home in almost any undisturbed landscape of the islands. They

FOLLOWING PAGES: A Hawaiian Eden, Waipi'o Valley once was home to thousands on the Big Island. Today, seekers of a traditional life-style have restored and maintained taro patches to create an enclave of the past.

dominate both the upland and lowland rain forests, towering to a hundred feet. In bogs they shrink to bonsai size. The small leaves may be fuzzy or shiny. The flowers are mostly scarlet, but some mavericks have blossoms that are yellow or orange. A botanical chameleon in the myrtle family, the ohia produces a wood so dense and hard that it once was shipped to the mainland for use as railroad ties. With good reason the ohia was given the name *Metrosideros polymorpha*—"core of iron, many forms."

My informant and guide was William P. Mull, a naturalist and photographer who has been campaigning to preserve native ecosystems in the islands for more than 20 years. Though vigorous and agile at 72, Bill uses a walking stick in the field, mostly, I think, to whack foreign plants. It's a symbolic act or a simple reflex action against newcomers that are threatening what is left of Hawaii's natural domains.

Alien plants haven't mastered the art of living on newly minted rock. This makes land like the 1855 lava among the most weed-free, pristine environments on the islands. But foreign species are invading and menacing most of Hawaii's last remaining natural habitats. Areas that escaped destruction by agriculture, grazing, and development are now threatened by aggressive species brought to the islands by man. Exotics such as banana poka vines from the Andes, fire trees from the Azores, and guavas from Brazil are crowding, smothering, and shading out native Hawaiian flora. In their home territories, these plants have natural enemies—insects, fungi, and other controls—to keep them in check. In Hawaii's gentle landscapes they run amok. Feral pigs and goats and deer multiply the damage, trampling and nibbling a unique biological heritage into extinction. Pigs further disrupt the landscape by rooting in the soil and dispersing unwanted seeds from the contents of their stomachs and the mud on their cloven feet.

But trespassers have not yet reached the montane forest in Kipuka 9. It still belongs to a dwindling, distinctly Hawaiian wilderness Bill wanted me to see. "Look how defenseless the native plants are," he said, as we plunged into the shadowy corridors of the kipuka. "These forest species evolved unbothered by large chomping and tromping mammals. That's why we have mintless mints, thornless raspberries, and nettleless nettles. There was nothing for them to jab or nettle, and these defense mechanisms slowly disappeared. Mints lost their chemical deterrent; raspberry bushes shed their thorns. Hawaiian species evolved with few predators and little competition. They can't contend with uncontrolled aliens, and so are losing out."

A medley of native plants grew on the ferny, mossy forest floor, but it was the lush tree ferns that overwhelmed my eyes. Long, curving fronds unfurling from trunks 10 to 15 feet tall bent into a lacy bower above our heads. Smaller ferns crowded the narrow trail. Their new growth was tinted a soft, salmon red that brought a blush to the relentless green.

Fallen trees and tree ferns shaggy with mosses and liverworts created an impenetrable grid of logs that nurtured ohia seedlings and other plants, including foot-long tongue ferns. High above, the ohias spread their twisting, silvery arms into airy crowns that formed open trellises against the sky. The sun flaring on the ferns suffused the understory with a soft light. Bill called it an upside-down rain forest, because the lushness and diversity of vegetation was not in the high canopy, as it is in the continental tropics, but in the zones below.

As we followed a narrow trail, Bill identified plants I had never seen: the *pa'iniu*, with rosettes of long, silvery, lilylike leaves; sweet-scented *maile*, the vine Hawaiians gather to make traditional leis; mountain *naupaka*, a sprawling shrub with a blossom that has a large gap between two petals, so it looks like a half-flower; clumps of *olonā*, whose stems produce the strongest natural fiber in the world. "Hawaiians used it to make fishlines that reputedly lasted so long they were given individual names and handed down from generation to generation," said Bill.

In the kipuka only the ohia had conspicuous flowers—a scattering of red pompoms accenting the crown of gray-green. The mint had dainty, fuchsia blossoms, but they hung below the leaves, the better to be seen by their insect pollinators. The showy flowers that ornament gardens—fragrant pink or white plumeria and masses of flaming bougainvillea from the West Indies, gingers and orchids from Asia, and birds of paradise from Africa—arrived in the last 200 years. They are not part of a Hawaiian landscape that nature designed.

Bill's specialty is photographing tiny invertebrates such as the happyface spider, which has markings on its quarter-inch-long back that are a caricature of a grinning human. As we walked along, Bill stopped beside some plants, methodically turning over leaves. Finally he found what he was searching for. It looked like a tiny bump on a leaf. Through his magnifying glass I saw that it was a green caterpillar, about half an inch long. It had minuscule claws on its front legs, which were holding a fly almost as large as itself. The dark, hairline stripe down its translucent body was fly-matter moving through the inchworm's gut. It was the notorious killer caterpillar, unique to the Hawaiian islands. Carnivorous caterpillars exist in other places, but only in Hawaii do they actually ambush prey, seizing them in lightning-fast strikes.

We explored amid a chorus of birdsong, which added a sweet gaiety to the forest. We heard the *'i'iwi*, the *'apapane*, and the *'ōma'o*—Hawaiian birds that have found havens in ancient, upper-elevation forests.

Many species of Hawaiian forest birds are living on borrowed time, clinging to existence in the remaining woodlands. In fact, they are disappearing at the highest rate of any endangered birds in the world. Biologists estimate that about 80 percent of Hawaii's original bird species have disappeared since the arrival of humans. Some were improbable creatures, like the flightless geese and ducks that survived well into Polynesian times. They stood three or four feet tall and weighed some twenty-five pounds.

Bird species have disappeared because vanishing forests robbed them of a place to live. The ancient Hawaiians, who slashed and burned the lower forests to make way for their gardens and breadfruit groves, destroyed the habitat of birds, which also were killed for food and for their feathers.

By the time Capt. James Cook, the English navigator, came upon what he named the Sandwich Islands in 1778, at *(Continued on page 50)*

Gnarled ohia tree towers above a patch of vegetation untouched by a lava flow on the Big Island. Such oases, called kipukas, isolate plants and animals, setting the stage for evolution of new species. Scarlet flowers of the ohia (opposite, left) bring color to Hawaii's forests, deserts, and bogs. A long, curved bill enables the ʻiʻiwi *(opposite) to sip nectar from tubular flowers. This once-plentiful bird belongs to the honeycreeper family, which diversified in Hawaii into more than 50 species.*

A caricature of a human face smiles from the back of a Hawaiian happyface spider (opposite and below). This tiny species rests on the undersides of leaves during the day. At night it clings to silk strands that pick up the vibrations of an approaching insect. Then the bristly legs of the spider pull sticky silk from its spinnerets to entangle its prey. Spiders first reached Hawaii as hatchlings carried aloft on the breeze-catching strands of silk or by hitching a ride on birds.

WILLIAM P. MULL (OPPOSITE AND ABOVE)

Nemesis of native insect life, alien big-headed ants attack a carnivorous caterpillar as it grasps a leaf with its hind legs (opposite, left). Social insects originally from Africa, the ants attack in numbers (opposite), using mandibles to bleed and weaken their prey (above). Hawaiian insects have not evolved defenses against these pests, which have virtually exterminated many native species that once pollinated plants and provided food for birds.

least 32 species of unique Hawaiian birds had disappeared. Their bones have been recovered by the thousand from sand dunes, sinkholes, and household middens, and they document the existence of bizarre flightless ducks, rails, geese, ibises with tiny wings, and long-legged, bird-eating owls.

Then, in the early 19th century, the Hawaiian nobility took the destruction of habitat upland in the quest for sandalwood, a tree prized in China for its fragrance and used for furniture and incense. At first the great King Kamehameha held a royal monopoly, and he financed the guns he used in the conquest of the islands with the sale of the logs to white traders. When he died in 1819, lesser chiefs embarked on a frenzied plunder of sandalwood to trade with China. In a rush to acquire personal luxuries, they decimated the forests, forcing their subjects to cut the trees and haul the timber tied on their backs to the waiting ships.

On a visit to Hawaii's Kohala district in 1823, the missionary William Ellis encountered villages "destitute of inhabitants, except a few women," because the people were in the mountains felling sandalwood trees. By 1840 the hillsides had been virtually denuded, and the trade ended.

Cattle also were culprits. They came to the island of Hawaii in 1793 and 1794 aboard the ships of the British navigator Capt. George Vancouver as gifts to Kamehameha. This revered king, who united the islands under his rule, placed a ten-year *kapu,* or taboo, on killing cattle, and they roamed unrestrained and multiplied. By 1823 their population was so large that missionary Ellis referred to "immense herds." It was well into the 20th century before ranchers tracked down most of the feral cattle. In the meantime these animals, along with feral sheep and goats, converted woodlands to open plains. Forests shrank even further when investors from the mainland discovered that low-lying terrain was ideal for sugarcane.

I saw what damage grazing had done to the upper slopes of Mauna Kea on my way to the Hakalau Forest National Wildlife Refuge, a preserve that protects dense populations of native forest birds. A somber mist swallowed the broad views and reduced the occasional koa and *māmane* trees to spectral shadows. Only the tall thickets of gorse stood forth, taking possession of that gray realm with their springtime blaze of yellow flowers.

"Gorse probably came into the islands tangled in the wool of sheep sometime before 1920," said refuge manager Dick Wass. "During the early years, its spread was limited by browsing sheep. But when sheep were replaced by cattle at mid-century, the gorse infestation exploded because cattle don't eat it."

A stately acacia sometimes called Hawaiian mahogany, koa provides the mainstay of the '*akiapola'au*'s diet. This small yellow bird depends on older trees with large, decaying branches that harbor insect larvae in the bark. The bird's dual-purpose bill is ingeniously adapted for getting this food. Its stubby lower mandible chips away the bark, woodpecker style, and then the bird hooks out the insects with a long, curved upper bill.

Like many of its cousins in the diverse honeycreeper family, the 'akiapola'au may have become too specialized for its own good, and disease and the decline of koa forests have all but annihilated this remarkable little bird with its Swiss-army-knife bill.

Dick Wass and his refuge staff are implementing a koa protection plan. They are getting rid of feral pigs and cattle and controlling such introduced weeds as banana poka, gorse, and Florida blackberry, which compete with native plants for space, sunlight, and nutrients. They also are planting koa seedlings—126,000 between 1992 and 1997. Perhaps their efforts can keep the ʻakiapolaʻau from going extinct.

All the Hawaiian honeycreepers, or *Drepanidinae,* that have ever lived share a common finchlike ancestor. They fanned out and diversified into dozens of species and subspecies that are now down to 26, with 16 classified as endangered. In just a few million years, descendants developed differences in shape, size, color, and bill to make the most of their habitat and to take advantage of the plants they found. The ʻiʻiwi, for example, in an exquisite example of form following function, has a long, curving bill that fits its favorite nectar-flower like a finger fitting a glove.

With ornithologist Jack Jeffrey I stalked the ʻiʻiwi and other birds in the large stand of ohias that is the hallmark of the refuge's Puaʻākala tract. We were in high country at 6,400 feet, and myriad tiny birds were trilling, twittering, and squeaking in a canopy ablaze with scarlet flowers. Jack briefed me on the birds as we strolled under the trees, stopping to listen to each song.

The ballad of an ʻiʻiwi consists of sharp whistles and sounds like the creakings of a rusty swing. But the bird's beauty makes up for what it lacks in musical talent. The ʻiʻiwi are scarlet bundles of energy, flitting from flower to flower, restlessly flicking their jet-black wings.

Even with field glasses the birds were hard to see, for they generally kept to the very tops of the trees and never came down to the ground. Now and then they alighted on a lower branch, winking with color like fragments of stained glass. There were red ʻapapane, orange *ʻākepa,* yellow *ʻamakihi,* and scarlet ʻiʻiwi. With these diminutive birds glimmering in the blossoming trees and their calls shimmering in the air, the damp, chill mountainside was transformed.

But a new, unseen enemy stalks the birds in the Puaʻākala tract. That silent invader is disease.

Scientists have found evidence that the birds of Puaʻākala have been exposed to introduced avian malaria and bird pox. Hawaiian forest birds have little resistance to these diseases and succumb as the Hawaiians themselves perished from measles and influenza epidemics in the 19th century. Until now, birds at high elevations have escaped these plagues, which are transmitted by mosquitoes. The pests arrived in Hawaii as stowaways in the 1820s and swarmed across the lowlands, breeding epidemics, but elevations above 6,000 feet have remained mosquito-free.

Are the Puaʻākala birds being exposed to disease by going down to lower elevations, or have the mosquitoes become acclimated to the higher elevations and cooler temperatures? "We don't know what is going on," says Rebecca Cann, the University of Hawaii geneticist who detected the problem. "We can easily become too complacent thinking everything will take care of itself if we protect the habitat."

It is a hostile, hazardous world for Hawaii's birds of the forest. They have been besieged by diseases and deprived of habitat. Evolving in isolation and away from mammalian predators, they are vulnerable to such aliens as mongooses, feral cats, and rats and lose out when they compete with birds new to the islands, such as the aggressive Indian myna and Japanese white-eye. In fact, there are few native land birds left in the lowlands. Unless conservation efforts succeed in protecting the survivors in the uplands, the last of these distinctive beings will be in great danger of extinction.

Above 12,000 feet on Mauna Kea's windswept expanses, where winter storms bring deep snows, virtually nothing grows. Cinder cones the color of burnt brick stand like massive dead embers over the rough, gray terrain. Glacial rubble is massed in smaller piles, a product of colder times, when the summit was buried in ice. Lake Waiʻau occupies the crater of a cinder cone, but it seems out of place, like a puddle in the Sahara. On this lunar landscape, the Mauna Kea Observatory complex, with its gleaming domes, looks like a space station of the future.

People regularly ski on Mauna Kea, sometimes into early summer, but drought deprived me of that remarkable experience. I made up for it one evening by star-gazing above the clouds on the summit, beneath the same shining heavens that guided Polynesian navigators. As the sun sank, it flooded the horizon with a fiery glow and tinted the cloud layer pink, mauve, and then lavender before all color seeped away into darkness.

Stars began to multiply until the whole immense bowl of the sky was spangled with flecks and points of radiant light. There was a sharp clarity to the stars and the round, gleaming planets. But the galaxies made their appearance as luminous clouds—incandescent mists casting glory across the heavens from the far reaches of the universe.

The summit was a place of grand vistas, but there was also a hidden world at my feet. For years scientists shared the views of 19th-century botanist David Douglas, who described the region above 12,000 feet as a place with a "death-like stillness...not an animal or insect to be seen...not a blade of grass." Not until the late 1970s did entomologists Frank Howarth and Steven Lee Montgomery of the Bishop Museum prove otherwise. They found a simple ecosystem based on a food supply that is swept up the mountain by the wind.

"The best place to find the inhabitants is along the melting edge of a snowbank," said Steve. He explained why. When insects get blown up the mountain and land on the sun-warmed rocks, some are able to take off. But those that land on snow become numb from cold and die. So during the daytime thaw the newly discovered *wēkiu* bug and spider predators wait for their dinner to fall out of the refrigerator onto the moist rocks.

I never managed to find a wēkiu bug, but I have a certain admiration for the creatures that have made themselves at home in the thin air and Mauna Kea's cold, harsh wastes.

Long before astronomers and biologists began making trips to the summit, Hawaiian craftsmen climbed to this silent place to get the densest fine-grained basaltic lava for their adzes, their basic tools for working with wood. The quarry region, which extends across seven and a half square miles, is littered with mounds of blue-black flake debris and larger hammerstones. The site represents an incredible amount of labor. And for the Hawaiians, lightly dressed in tapa, or bark cloth, and wearing ti-leaf sandals and rain capes, toiling atop Mauna Kea must have been like a stint on Alaska's North Slope.

For a sense of how Hawaii used to be, I set off for the Waipi'o Valley, which begins where the Hāmākua coast road ends in a little park. From there the land drops sharply for nearly a thousand feet. From the park overlook, I gazed down on an emerald landscape as fresh and verdant as Eden. Serenity emanated from the valley, which seemed still except for a Hawaiian hawk catching thermals and soaring on air currents above the cliffs. Shaggy ironwood trees marked the boundary of the black-sand beach, where steep waves spent their strength in ruffles of foam. Beyond Waipi'o, the shoreline was a succession of cliffs and valleys as far as I could see.

"In the old days, Waipi'o was one continuous garden, mostly taro, with some bananas and sugarcane. In the 1800s, the Chinese arrived and planted some rice. But all these guava and mango and monkeypod trees came later," said Roy Toko, a driver with the Waipi'o Shuttle Service.

Roy considers himself more Hawaiian than anything else, though he's also part Japanese and part Chinese. Like many islanders, Roy speaks of himself as a "chop suey," a mix of several nationalities. He remembers when hundreds of people lived in the valley. There were churches, bars, a school, and a mill where the purplish corm of the taro plant was ground and turned into a bland pink paste called poi. The roads were mere easements for mules and horses, and there was always time to stop and "talk story."

That life-style disappeared with a 1946 tsunami, when huge waves roared about a mile inland and swept away everything in their path. The villagers had no warning, but no lives were lost. Even so, the disaster produced a mass exodus. "Now most of us live topside, but it is nice to see more and more families going down and opening taro patches," said Roy. "The valley is slowly returning to taro."

Today about 50 people live permanently in the valley. Some of the residents are local old-timers; some are younger people from Honolulu and the mainland, who, as one observer put it, live "long-hair, escapist style." There's Tom Araki, a short, wispy man with a drooping white moustache who presides over a five-room guest house. It has no hot water or electricity, but in the evening, when Tom lights the kerosene lamps, there is fruit from his garden on tables on the veranda and a silence that carries the soft melody of the wind in the trees.

Jack Kaholoaa, who says the best thing about the valley is that there are no policemen, works for Sherri Hannum. Originally from Missouri, Sherri operates trail rides in the valley.

But the man I had come to see was Kia Fronda, who keeps Hawaiian culture alive by living it. A short but commanding figure with a black beard and dark, piercing eyes, he is a Vietnam War veteran and a graduate of the University of Hawaii. He came to Waipi'o to live close to the earth on his grandfather's land. With the help of family and friends, he restored the irrigation channels. He replanted the taro patches and created a lovely tropical setting, lush with flowers, fruit trees, and native healing herbs.

"I use this place to teach a love and respect for the land and to educate young people to Hawaiian traditions. We need an awareness of where we come from. Without our heritage we are weak and vulnerable, like a tree without strong roots," said Kia, as we walked the narrow dikes enclosing each flooded taro patch.

One plot, covered with arrowhead-shaped leaves the size of platters, was ready for harvest. Another had just been sown, and the leaf stems stood in neat rows in the dark water. We stayed for a while looking out across the flooded fields, hearing the trickle of water moving through the irrigation ditches and the hoarse call of a black-crowned night heron flying low with a lazy flapping of wings. It was as if I had stepped into the past: a Hawaii of chiefs in feathered capes and helmets, of joyous harvest festivals, when war was taboo, and taro, called *kalo* in Hawaiian, was the staff of life.

In the *Kumulipo,* the Hawaiian chant of creation, the first-born of the progenitor of mankind dies. After the child is buried, it grows into the first taro plant. "Taro, or kalo, is our brother or sister. It is our connection to the land," says Kia. For Kia and for others like him, taro has become a symbol of the Hawaiian renaissance, summarized in the bumper sticker: Live Hawaiian Culture, Plant Kalo.

When I first met Kia he was teaching two young men to weave palm-frond baskets. We were downstairs in a large room with a kitchen and no walls. "Auntie Darling"—Sara de los Santos—who has been strumming a ukulele for 60 years, was playing and singing. While we listened, dancers from Oahu and a local hula *halau,* or group, were getting ready to perform. Then outside on a grassy lawn, as Kia beat a strong rhythm on a gourd drum, they tried new steps, made mistakes, and tried again, laughing in the fine, misty rain.

Sometimes groups of youngsters stay for several days at Kia's place, learning dances and singing old chants. He teaches the importance of sharing and how to take from the land and how to give back.

"Waipi'o means curving water, but it refers to more than the streams meandering down the valley," said Kia. "Waipi'o means the whole cycle of rain: water seeping through the earth and draining to the sea, where it evaporates and brings rain back to the sky.

"Anyone may perceive the beauty of this valley, but you won't understand Waipi'o until you live and feel a part of the cycle of curving waters."

It was raining when I left Kia's place. The thousand-foot walls that enclose the valley on three sides were tinseled with waterfalls. The puddles on the paths had become murmuring streams. The raindrops beat a tattoo in the trees. The voices of Waipi'o were singing.

Waterfalls and pale foliage of kukui trees brighten the headwall of Molokai's Halawa Valley. Ancient Hawaiians cultivated such wet, windward valleys, initiating an era of rapid change in the ecology of the islands.

In a typical Hawaiian rain forest scene, apple-green hapu'u *tree ferns shade the ground in the Nature Conservancy's Kamakou Preserve on Molokai. The fronds fan out from the tops of fuzzy stems as much as 20 feet tall. Hapu'u forms a dense second canopy below gnarled ohias that dominate the forest's upper story. The slow-growing fern begins life as a coiled fiddlehead (above). Feral pigs threaten forests by trampling and uprooting vegetation and dispersing seeds of alien plants.*

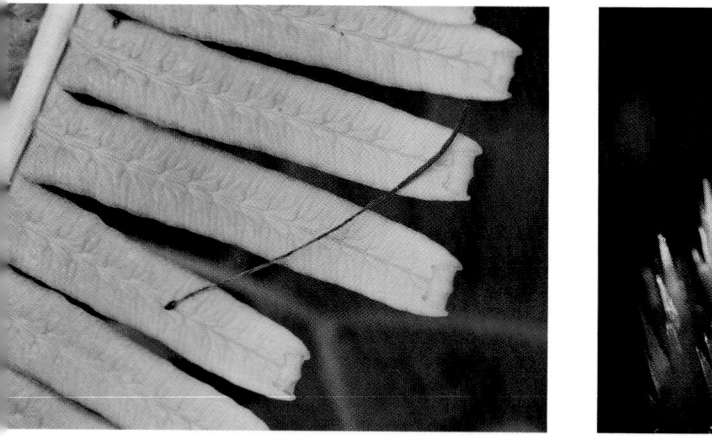

In Molokai's Kamakou Preserve, shiny berries of makole *poke through ground cover. A small, succulent herb and member of the coffee family, makole commonly creeps along damp forest floors. Its presence is indicative of no pig damage, for it can't survive in disturbed soil. A filament-like stamen from an ohia flower (opposite, left) adds a red accent to an* uluhe *fern. Opposite, yellow spikes pop up from a bed of moss in Kamakou's wetlands, a major watershed for the island. To safeguard this critical area, the Conservancy established Kamakou in 1982.*

An Asian tiger mosquito alights near the eye of a scarlet 'apapane. *Diseases such as avian malaria and pox, carried by other species of mosquitoes that were accidentally introduced into the islands in the early 19th century,*

have contributed to the decline of Hawaiian bird populations. Clearing of forest for lumber and agriculture destroyed their habitat. Feral goats, deer, and cattle and exotic birds from the continents also have disrupted the native ecosystems.

FRANS LANTING / MINDEN PICTURES

Once near extinction, the Hawaiian goose, or nene (below), has increased in number as a result of a captive breeding program. Flocks had dwindled as hunters slaughtered the birds for food, and mongooses preyed especially upon such ground-nesting species. A voracious predator introduced to control rats in sugarcane fields, a mongoose (opposite) grasps an ʻapapane.

FOLLOWING PAGES: *Blending in with the rocky landscape, a marine crab ventures above waterline on Molokai's Moʻomomi Preserve.*

There are many ways to start the day on Maui, but I can think of none better than standing on the rim of Haleakala Crater watching sunlight spread across the vast, stony basin far below. In the dry, clear, cold at 10,000 feet, a landscape of sinuous contours takes shape. Cinder cones of perfect symmetry emerge from the haze. The light flaring on them reveals somber red, copper, and yellow tones—colors of fire blazoning the volcanic essence of the place. Dunes of cinder and ash fall away from the summit in long billows. Dark gulches crease the crater walls, which are scalloped with fans of pale talus at their base. Nothing moves in this surreal creation, but the composition of color, shadow, and form is as stark and stunning as a Bartók concerto.

Looking down on the crater's uncommon landmarks provides more than a glorious view. It arouses curiosity and expectations, for its unique precincts promise things unforeseen and utterly new.

The landscape that seems so barren from the rim is full of surprises. Owls hunt during the day; māmane trees flourish even in drought, capturing moisture from fog; seabirds fly up to the high mountain desert after dark; unorthodox geese called nene live on the land, do not migrate long distances, and, through evolution, have lost half the webbing on their feet; and unusual silverswords produce scimitar-shaped leaves that form globes gleaming with a frosted light on the cinder soil.

So it was with great anticipation that I began a ten-mile hike down into and across the oval crater. The basin, slightly smaller than Manhattan, is one part of Haleakala National Park. Another consists of the steep, forested Kīpahulu Valley, which descends the crater's outer slopes to the sea in stream-cut gorges opulent with waterfalls and tropical growth.

Cathleen Natividad Hodges, endangered species project leader for the park, was waiting for me at headquarters a few miles below Pu'u 'Ula'ula, the volcano's 10,023-foot summit. Of special interest to this petite scientist is the *'ua'u,* or Hawaiian dark-rumped petrel, a now rare seabird that nests inland, flying upward thousands of feet to occupy hollows and crevices in the great emptiness of the crater rim. Cathleen and her staff monitor more than 500 burrows, checking on the ocean wanderers from the time the adults return each year in March until the young fly off to sea in October. Her map of sites represents many years of work scouring the slopes for fresh bird droppings, which mark the area of a nest.

It was early March, and a few petrels were already in residence, waiting in their burrows for their mates and for the mating season to begin. Cathleen invited me along as she made her rounds.

Rain Forest

NIIHAU
KAUAI
OAHU
MOLOKAI
MAUI
LANAI
KAHOOLAWE
HAWAII

"We know very little about where these petrels go when they are living at sea. On shore the adults return to the same burrow year after year, traveling alone but faithful to the same mates."

Cathleen had arranged a flimsy obstacle made of seven toothpicks in front of each opening. "It's our high-tech way of determining if a burrow is in use."

At burrow number 90, the barricade had collapsed. Lying flat on the ground, I used a flashlight to peer inside. A bird was sitting very still. Its white forehead accentuated the hooked, black bill surmounted by nose tubes. Like many seabirds, petrels drink seawater and excrete the excess salt in their blood through nostrils atop their beaks.

Petrels are more heard than seen, for they come and go only at night. Their repeated call, a long moan ascending into a yip, ripples eerily through the darkness, but as the birds approach their nests they grow silent. Then the only sound is the whoosh of their long, tapered wings.

These birds were once abundant on all the main islands except Niihau. First the species was hit hard by the ancient Hawaiians, who considered the chicks a delicacy—a treat reserved for their chiefs. Later the Indian mongoose threatened the petrels. A weasel-like predator, it was imported late in the 19th century to rid the cane fields of rats. It was a misguided scheme, because rats are mostly nocturnal and the mongoose is diurnal. But the mongoose thrived, eating the eggs and young of Hawaii's ground-nesting birds instead of rats. Meanwhile the petrels have suffered a tragic decline that has put them on the federal endangered species list.

They have started making a comeback as a result of the park's feral animal and predator control policies. Part of Cathleen's program involves setting and monitoring traps for mongooses as well as for feral cats and dogs. She is also trying to check the population explosion of alien yellow jackets, using a poisoned bait. Nothing, however, has been found to contain the spread of the aggressive Argentine ant, a ravenous creature that preys on the larvae of native ground-nesting bees and is also threatening other native insect populations. At risk is the lovely silversword, which depends on native insect pollinators for its survival.

The Haleakala silversword grows only on the dry subalpine slopes of

FOLLOWING PAGES: Wailua Falls filigrees a forest glen on windward Maui. Many of Hawaii's endemic plants thrive in the damp upper fern-and-forest belt between the sun-blasted crater of Haleakala and surf-drenched coves.

the crater, enduring a tough environment that few other plants could take.

"It's summer every day and winter every night, with high levels of solar radiation, low humidity, and desiccating winds," says Art Medeiros, a biologist at the park. "The plant also puts up with cinder soil that is poor in nutrients and as abrasive as broken glass."

Art speaks enthusiastically about the silversword's genius for survival. Consider the wizardry of the stiff leaves: They fan out and form a living bowl that acts to gather water, which the plant stores in a gel-like substance; they make a mulch, putting down a ring of dead leaves around the plant; their curve deflects the wind, as does their strategy of growing close to the ground. The silvery hairs are also multipurpose, providing wind protection, screening ultraviolet rays, condensing moisture from fog, and protecting the plant from cold and heat.

But when I saw the silverswords, I marveled more at their beauty than at their fortitude or engineering. I had entered the crater on the Sliding Sands Trail with Cathleen. Once beyond the observation areas on the rim, no one else was in sight. We had been hiking downhill for almost an hour, kicking up puffs of dust from the loose cinders and ash underfoot. Our steps were a counterpoint to a silence so dense it could be felt.

My eyes were tracing the dark emptiness of an old lava flow when I saw the gleam of silverswords in the distance, scattered like sequins across a drab brown slope. Close up, the leaves were pale green; only the down was silvery. Their shape was graceful, like large dahlias sprung full-blown from the gritty ground—Cinderellas of the botanical world.

Silverswords are even more flamboyant in bloom, sending up a single mighty stalk as much as seven feet, sumptuous with hundreds of maroon flower heads. Flowering lasts for several weeks, but after the plant sets seed, it withers and dies. It may take as few as two years or as many as fifty for a silversword to grow from seed to flowering. No one knows what makes them flower, but some years they go off in much larger numbers than in others.

To scientists, the daisylike blooms coated with a sticky resin are a clue to the silversword's humble ancestry—a California tarweed in the composite, or sunflower, family. Enzyme analysis also shows that the tarweed is chemically kin to the silversword. Nature went on a spree when this colonist landed in Hawaii, for it diversified into 3 genera containing 28 species. The descendants provide perhaps the foremost example of adaptive radiation in the plant kingdom.

In 1874 Isabella Bird saw thousands of silverswords, "their cold, frosted silver gleam making the hill-side look like winter or moonlight." In the years that followed, they were yanked up by the thousand for ornaments; they were rolled down the slopes for sport; and goats gobbled them like candy. By the 1920s, the silversword was in danger of extinction.

Without the efforts of men like Ted Rodrigues, it would be a memory. Haleakala's feral animal control supervisor, Ted is dedicated to eliminating goats from the park. "Vegetarian piranhas," he calls them.

More than 17,000 goats have been removed over the years in organized hunts. Fencing them out, a project that lasted 11 years, ended in

1987. A recent count put the number of silverswords at 50,000. Setting miles of fencing on terrain "only a mountain goat could love" has been a formidable undertaking. Helicopters haul the supplies and tools, dropping them on the rim, where work crews set posts and string wire while balancing on the near-vertical slopes.

"There are fewer than a dozen goats left in the crater," said Ted. "Five are ones we introduced. They have collars with radio transmitters, so we can easily track them. Since goats are very sociable, these beeping Judas goats lead us to any arrivals that may come through breaks in the fences."

Ted had been waiting for Cathleen and me along the trail near the Pu'u o Pele cinder cone. He is a strong man with a trim black beard and an Iberian face that would be at home in a Velázquez painting. His ancestors were part of the tide of Portuguese immigrants who came from the Azores to work as contract laborers on the sugar plantations. Cathleen inherited her sloe-eyed, dainty beauty from her Japan-born mother.

Raised in Hawaii, it was natural for Ted and Cathleen to speak in the lilting accents of Hawaiian pidgin, a language that evolved as Hawaiians and immigrants from China, Japan, Portugal, the Philippines, and the Azores worked together. It's a language that has a faster, more direct way of saying things. *Da kine* refers to whatever is at hand, so offering someone fruit in a bowl becomes "You want da kine?" *Pau* is the term for finish, now used even when speaking perfect English, but I needed a translation for *Bym bye pau,* which means "By and by this problem or difficulty will pass."

Like most visitors to Maui, I had wrongly assumed Haleakala Crater was formed by volcanic activity. In fact, the credit goes to the forces of erosion. Rains and mountain torrents had carved two great oval depressions that were once 6,000 feet deep—deeper than the Grand Canyon—and also cut two breaches in the crater rim. Later eruptions flooded the basin with lava, cinders, and ash and filled in 3,000 feet.

Just off the main trail, which parallels the cliffs, we came to a gnarled outcrop of lava near one of the cinder cones. On a natural platform someone had recently placed an offering: The flowers were withered, but the pineapple was still intact. It was a simple but poignant tribute to the sanctity of the place, a reverence that goes back to ancient times.

Legend says it was at Haleakala that the demigod Maui snared Lā, the sun. He did not let go until he extracted a promise that the sun would move more slowly across the heavens, giving humans longer days to do their work. Hence the name Hale a ka Lā—House of the Sun.

The crater floor is dotted with prehistoric cairns, platforms, and rock shelters. Archaeologists have located quarries used by adz makers and have found natural slingstones that may have been weapons for hunting petrels and nene. In the past, Hawaiians came to the crater to inter bones of their dead, which were venerated as a source of mana, or divine power. Hawaiians also came to the crater to perform ceremonies and to study the stars. Ted remembered an old *kahuna,* a traditional priest, telling him many years ago of observing the night sky from inside the crater of a cinder cone. Watching the stars as they passed over the rim produced a calendar marking the seasons for farmers, fishermen, and religious events.

On the trail, plants became more abundant the farther we went. The juniper-like pūkiawe grew thicker, lusher, and more bountiful with white, pink, or red berries. *Kūpaoa,* a twiggy relative of the silversword, stood a little taller, its branches crowned with a nest of leaves at the tip. *Pilo,* a plant of the coffee family with orange berries, bracken fern, and a dainty, low-growing geranium with silvery leaves made their appearance.

Clouds were flowing like a river through the Kaupō Gap ahead, and their swirling performance—an integral part of Haleakala landscapes—held my gaze. Though they poured into the crater in a thick, cottony cascade, they evaporated in the crater's dry heat. A gauzy cloud drifted above a cinder cone like a tendril of smoke and then melted away without a trace.

Sometimes the clouds have more stamina, and they coalesce and solidify. Mark Twain described a "ghostly procession" that "blended together till the abyss was stored to the brim with a fleecy fog." But my day was filled with blazing sunshine, and the bleak stretch of rough, fragmented a'a lava we crossed after lunch radiated heat like a stove.

The landscape changed again as we neared Palikū, where the lava was older and the rainfall was more plentiful. We passed 'ōhelo, with leaves bitten red by frost, and ohia and sandalwood. Shrubs such as the *'a'ali'i* grew to tree height. Its name comes from the term for Hawaiian aristocracy, for the long, narrow leaves grow upright, standing erect even in wind with a certain dogged nobility. Evening primroses patterned the ground with clumps of yellow blossoms that luminesced like Spanish doubloons in the waning light.

The scraggly māmane trees grew more patriarchal, and their clusters of narrow, wispy leaves created dappled patterns of shade. Prized by Hawaiians for its hard, durable wood and by the goats for its tender leaves, the māmane was reduced almost to oblivion.

The endangered Hawaiian goose, or nene, which is native to only two islands, Hawaii and Maui, faced a similar plight. It was slaughtered for meat to provision the whaling ships that made the town of Lahaina, on Maui, their main port of call in the mid-Pacific between the 1840s and the 1860s. Hunting the nene was not banned until 1911, but by then the voracious mongoose was also speeding their decline. Numbers plummeted from an estimated 25,000 in the 18th century to fewer than 50 birds on the Big Island in 1960. On Maui they were actually extinct.

Then in a joint international rescue program, the Division of Fish and Game and the Wildfowl Trust, (a breeding refuge in Slimbridge, England) began rearing nene for release in *(Continued on page 82)*

Crown of blossoms six feet tall tops a Haleakala silversword, an endemic plant that grows only on Maui's dry upper heights. As rarely as once in 50 years, the plant sends up one magnificent stalk, then dies.

FOLLOWING PAGES: A thin ribbon far below the morning clouds, a valley stream rushes seaward through mountainous west Maui.

The differing faces of Maui rain forests: Deep in one, huge platterlike leaves of the endemic herb ʻapeʻape *(right) cap thick stems that may rise four feet from the forest floor. Leaves sometimes measure three feet in diameter and serve comfortably as umbrellas. Above, Puʻu Eke, a volcanic dome 4,480 feet high, was built of three superposed lava flows in west Maui. Barely visible from the air, diminutive growth—an elfin cloud forest—patches its ancient slopes. Bog pools and pocks on its summit hold and drain surface water that seeps downward, feeding cool springs at its base.*

FRANS LANTING / MINDEN PICTURES

Naturalist Bill Evanson inspects vegetation torn and trampled by one

of the worst threats to Hawaii's magnificent native forests—feral pigs.

Pig hunters climb past sharp-pointed bursts of sisal, an introduced plant, near Molokai's Pelekunu Valley. One hunter, Kimo Naki (opposite), shows off the results of a successful hunt. A hundred thousand feral pigs roam the Hawaiian islands. Most of the dark, bristly beasts are a cross between Polynesian pigs and domestic animals. The creatures dig up soil and vegetation to get at roots and worms, and carry seeds from place to place.

the wild. Since 1962 more than 2,000 captive nene have been reintroduced into the crater's lusher eastern end and to another ancestral home on the Big Island. Restocking did not always take. Some birds did not breed; eggs did not always hatch; and many goslings did not survive. But about 200 nene now promenade around the crater's eastern end, and some 350 more inhabit Hawaii Volcanoes National Park.

The weather at Palikū can be biting cold, but that evening was crisp and pleasant. Sunset added a gloss to the sere grasses at the base of a thousand-foot *pali,* or cliff. The nene were easy to approach, for they have no fear of people. There was a constant low gabbling as they waddled across the rock-strewn meadow, muttering as they walked. The continual sounds may be the way the birds keep track of one another.

The next day, in the pale light of early morning, the nene took short flights, circling in pairs and honking, with softer sounds than their distant cousins, Canada geese. A solitary native short-eared owl glided in a circle. Suddenly it dived and then headed toward the cliffs, presumably carrying a rat, mouse, or chukar back to its young. Fossil bones of this owl date back a mere 1,500 years. Evidently this partially diurnal species took up residence in Hawaii only after there were Polynesian rats available as prey.

The cliffs at Palikū often are shrouded in thick mist as clouds spill over from the windward slopes of Haleakala. But even on days of luminous clarity, there are usually a few clouds writhing down like incense from the heights, conjuring an aura of mystery. The walls of the Kalapawili Ridge seem like a mighty citadel guarding a Shangri-la. You can't help wondering what's on the other side.

I was transported there on the magic carpet of the modern world, whisked up from the crater by helicopter and flown over the pali wall to the remote upper Kīpahulu Valley. Ravines dissect its steep, matted slopes, turning them into almost impenetrable tracts where uncommon plants abide. Rare birds flit among the mossy ohia branches. Knife-edge ridges channel torrential rains—as much as 400 inches a year—into thundering waterfalls and rivers that intensify the sense of remoteness of the place.

I was in the company of resource management specialist Steve Anderson, a lanky botanist who began working for the park in 1983. Steve is a haole, a word everyone uses to refer to a white person. The etymology of the term suggests it means "without breath." Perhaps it originally referred to a person who did not need to take a deep breath to chant his genealogy as Hawaiians did. In other words, a person lacking a long pedigree.

"We've stepped back in time to a Hawaii that is as wild as when the first Marquesans came ashore," said Steve, after the helicopter whirled off to supply a crew repairing fences. The actively managed, near-pristine Kīpahulu tract was donated to Haleakala National Park in 1969 by the Nature Conservancy and the state. To keep the upper valley intact, it is maintained as a research reserve generally open only to bona fide scientists.

Before my eyes could register the details of the scene, I was distracted by the melodies that rippled through the forest in a fugue of warbles, whistles, chirps, and trills. "It's early, so we're hearing many birds because they're out getting insects for their young," said Steve, as we gazed up at the airy ohia canopy, while birdsong and sunlight sifted down upon us.

Several species of honeycreepers with their specialized bills were fluttering among branches as high as 40 feet. I recognized a scarlet ʻiʻiwi. "With such long beaks, you wonder how they can fly," remarked Steve.

He sighted a Maui creeper, which he compared to a yellow tennis ball. We failed to see the largest bird, the *ʻākohekohe,* or crested honeycreeper, a striking creature with dark plumage flecked with orange and a crest of feathers on its forehead. They were once abundant on Molokai and Maui. Now only a small population survives and only in native rain forests on Haleakala. Other endangered honeycreepers have found sanctuary here: the Maui parrotbill, which hunts insects by snapping twigs with its beak; the *poʻouli,* a brown, stocky bird discovered as recently as 1973; and the seldom seen, greenish *nukupuʻu,* whose nest and young have never been described.

"We hope these birds can survive here in Kīpahulu, where the ecosystem is 100 percent native Hawaiian rain forest, with a full complement of native insects on which the young birds depend," Steve said.

We had started in an ohia forest at 6,500 feet and descended to 3,500 feet, where the stately koa shares the canopy with the ohia, flaunting clusters of sickle-shaped leaves. At least they look like leaves. To botanists they are flat, expanded stems called phyllodes that enable the tree to conserve water and reduce the stress from wind. But when koas are young and growing fast, they have finely divided, feathery leaves, efficient for gathering sunlight.

Though the ohia canopy is open, the understory is crowded with smaller trees and tree ferns with fronds that bend as you push past and then flap back. *ʻIe ʻie* vines twine around the trees and garland the branches with clusters of long, lilylike leaves that give the forest a festive look.

The forest floor itself is so choked with ferns, shrubs, and toppled trees burgeoning with mosses and sprouts that it forms a nearly impassable barrier. But not for feral pigs. They prefer easier paths, but they can plunge through the densest vegetation if they're hungry. Their assault is ferocious. In recent decades they have extended their range, plowing and grunting their way into the upper Kīpahulu Valley.

Dark, bristly beasts with up to four-inch tusks, they are a mix of pigs the Polynesians brought and the many domestic animals imported later. Scientists call them the worst scourge of Hawaiian forests. They cause damage by eating, uprooting, or trampling vegetation and by sowing the seeds of alien plants. Like Rototillers, they churn the ground to get at worms and roots, exposing the soil to rapid erosion that silts up streams and turns waterfalls into muddy flows that smother offshore reefs.

"The key to saving any Hawaiian forest is getting rid of the pigs. Here at the park we're building a whole series of fences to keep them out," said Steve, as I followed him on the narrowest of trails.

We were slogging through knee-high ground cover of stiff, scratchy *uluhe,* the false staghorn fern, which branches and rebranches relentlessly, spreading a rough, apple-green mat in all directions.

"Native trees can sprout up through uluhe, but where foreign grasses and weeds have taken hold in a disturbed area, the forest is finished, because the trees are not able to revegetate."

Steve worries about the vulnerability of Hawaii's remaining native flora and fauna, whose ranks grow thinner year by year. "Take the lobelias," he said, pointing to a plant with sprays of long, pink, tubular flowers fanning out from a waist-high rosette of long, green leaves. Like so much that is native to Hawaii, it was strangely beautiful and unlike any plant I had ever seen.

"That's the *Trematolobelia,* one of the plants from the family of lobeliads that has diversified into more than a hundred species. Twenty-five of these wonderful growth forms have gone extinct. All Hawaiian lobelias have weak stems and succulent leaves, which make them especially vulnerable to pigs. Several lobelias coevolved with some of the honeycreepers, so the curve of their flowers perfectly matches the curve of the bill. What happens to the birds when their nectar supply disappears? And what happens to the plants when the birds that disperse their seeds are gone?

"There's no place I know of in the United States that has the unique assemblage of plants and animals you find in Hawaii, and unfortunately pigs, goats, cattle, and the spread of introduced species are driving them to extinction. Some areas are too far gone to be saved, but here at Kīpahulu we have a good chance of preserving a special corner of the earth."

Before we left the upper Kīpahulu, we clambered along a boulder-strewn stretch of the Palikea stream. Sometimes the river roars with water, but drought had muted its voice as a diminished flow riffled over the smaller stones. Blue and red damselflies danced arabesques on gossamer wings. Native shrimp, which had returned from the sea and scaled waterfalls by climbing the wet mosses on the rocks, flicked their antennae as they picked their way around the quiet pools.

Our lure was a waterfall, which announced itself with a low rumble like the beat of muffled drums. Suddenly we rounded a meander and came to a cliff plastered with ferns and filigreed with water cascading down its broad face. Its spray descended upon us like a benediction. Rainbows, conjured from the mist by sunlight, shimmered in and out of existence.

Who knows how long we would have stayed, but our magic carpet could not be kept waiting.

I beheld another rainbow when I hiked out of the crater the following day, climbing the switchbacks on the Halemau'u Trail from the crater floor to the rim. I was above the clouds, and the sun was behind me. I looked down and saw my silhouette on the cloud bank below with a rainbow halo encircling my head. Scientists can explain the visual phenomenon known as the Brocken specter. To me it is part of the magic of Haleakala.

Deceptively delicate, a primitive small club moss—lepelepe-a-moa *in Hawaiian—is a surviving relative of scaly trees of the Carboniferous period 300 million years ago. Hawaiians braid it with rosebuds in making leis.*

On Maui's rooftop desert, the rim of Haleakala Crater catches the sunrise nearly two miles above the sea. Legend says the demigod Maui stood here and lassoed the sun to slow its track and gain more daylight; hence the Hawaiian name Hale a ka Lā—House of the Sun. Opposite, on the crater's floor, an endemic wolf spider carries her young papoose-style.

FOLLOWING PAGES: The most common native trees of Hawaii, ohias flourish on Haleakala's eastern slope.

TRANQUIL SHORES AND

He announced his presence with a plaintive song. She remained silent throughout his serenade, but perhaps she signaled her interest, for the next thing we knew he was by her side. We couldn't tell what made her so alluring, but in a few minutes she had also beguiled two other males. When they tried to intrude, the first suitor pushed and jostled the interlopers away. One of them persisted and charged his rival, propelling his great bulk out of the water and landing in a great geyser of spray. Again the first humpback whale drove his 40-ton rival back, but all we could actually see was a melee of splashing flippers and tail flukes.

"In these skirmishes competing humpback males whack each other with their powerful, 12-foot-wide tails or slam into each other in head-on collisions," said Dr. Paul Forestell, a scientist who has been studying the behavior of Hawaii's humpback whales since 1976.

"Before coming to blows, a male may try intimidating the competition by exaggerating his size. He gulps huge quantities of water or air, which balloons the accordion pleats along the throat and expands it into a pouch big enough to hold a small car. Sometimes the bluff works," said Paul.

I was aboard a Boston whaler in waters off Lanai with Paul, who is director of research and education for the Pacific Whale Foundation, one of the organizations studying these enormous marine mammals.

Suddenly, just over a hundred yards away, three wing-shaped tails appeared for a moment like giant dark moths above the water. After these fluke-up dives, all that remained on the choppy blueness were three round slicks, each a vortex of smooth water that scientists call "footprints," because they mark where a humpback has just been.

Paul thought the males were probably jockeying for position underwater, and whichever came up first to breathe would be the loser. But it was the female, a calf at her side, who appeared first. She took off, leading two of the contenders in a high-speed chase, swimming at the surface with her offspring and ardent swains trailing behind.

This hot pursuit is an important part of the courtship game for humpback whales, for it ensures that only the most fit whale of the group will mate with the female. We soon lost sight of the amorous entourage. Only one whale's misty spout hovered briefly above the water in a small cloud.

Paul started the motor, hoping to encounter more humpbacks in the Auau Channel between Lanai and Maui, a stretch of water eight miles wide that is referred to locally as a whale highway. Humpbacks in Hawaii once numbered an estimated 10,000. But decades of whaling decimated their numbers, and by 1976 fewer than a thousand were left. A protected species

MAGICAL SEAS

since 1966—by order of the International Whaling Commission—their numbers have greatly increased. Now every winter somewhere between 2,000 and 2,500 humpback whales migrate from their summer feeding grounds in the northern Pacific near Alaska across thousands of miles of ocean to reach the Hawaiian coast, where they breed and calve.

The whales favor the waters around Lanai, Maui, and Molokai, which have extensive shallows—defined as waters less than 100 fathoms, or 600 feet, deep. These are the preferred calving grounds, perhaps because the shallows provide some protection from sharks and have warmer water, which newborn whales may need.

A ringside seat to romance cetacean-style was part of the mix of adventure I encountered in Lanai's waters. Once referred to as the Pineapple Island and known as the world's largest pineapple plantation, Lanai was terra incognita for vacationers. Its iron-red earth was given over to ranching for nearly a hundred years, until Jim Dole bought 98 percent of the island's 90,000 acres in 1922. The Dole Company, Inc., which now has no connection with the Dole family, is the parent company, and it also owns many of the small bungalows in Lanai City, where nearly all of the 2,500 islanders live. The corporate owners have turned the economy away from pineapples and toward tourism, with the construction of two luxury resorts.

A few fishermen, backpackers, and divers have long enjoyed the unpublicized pleasures of Lanai's beaches and waters. During my stay, I explored reefs crowded not with snorkelers but with colorful fish flitting among the rocks and corals like gaudy butterflies. I strolled where no footprints marred the stretches of wind-rippled sand. And I skimmed a whale-shadowed indigo sea in a small boat, listening to the haunting songs of the humpback whales.

On that unforgettable day, Paul lowered a hydrophone into the water soon after we left the Mānele Small Boat Harbor on the southern coast of Lanai. Minutes later I heard a low rumble, like that of a motorboat: the sound of a humpback whale warming up and getting ready to sing, Paul said. I listened with amazement to the eerie, mournful song. The resonant, elongated moans, reedy creaks, and melodious sighs were unlike anything I had ever heard. There was an ineffable sadness to the song, like a dirge

FOLLOWING PAGES: A green sea turtle, beating its flippers like wings, glides beneath breaking surf. More than 90 percent of Hawaii's green sea turtles find their way to French Frigate Shoals in the Leeward Islands to breed.

DAVID DOUBILET

Ledges of lava serve as spillways for waves surging along the wild northwest

chanted by an unearthly being. A humpback's song is the loudest and most complex vocalization in the animal kingdom, according to Paul. In Hawaiian waters, humpback whales generally sing for six to thirty minutes at a time but sometimes for as long as two hours, repeating an intricate pattern of sounds and tones over and over. Singing seems to be a male prerogative and is done only in the mating season. But why they sing remains an intriguing mystery.

"It may well be to establish territory and warn other males away and to communicate with females across miles of ocean, telling them how big, how strong, and how sexy they are," said Paul.

As we crossed the Auau Channel, every horizon held mountains. At our back was Lanai's only peak, Lāna'ihale, its rounded crest marked with a ridge of Norfolk Island pines that looked like upright spears jabbed into the ground. Farther from shore, distance gave the island the simple silhouette of a smooth, low mound, and I could see why it was named Lanai, for the Hawaiian word means "swelling" or "hump." Molokai's mountains, ascending sharply from pale green shallows, demarcated the north. Directly ahead were the emerald uplands of west Maui, its beaches rimmed by the

RICHARD ALEXANDER COOKE III

coast of Molokai. Upwelling here stirs up nutrients, attracting plankton and fish.

skyscraper hotels of the Kā'anapali coast. To the southeast soared the mass of Maui's Haleakala volcano. Its graceful outline was broken by a necklace of clouds that piled up on the high slopes, leaving the disembodied summit afloat in the azure sky.

We never saw the whale that sang so poignantly of unfathomable things, for humpbacks sing only underwater.

Paul has observed them singing during some of his dives. "Each time, the whale was head down some 50 to 75 feet below the surface. With its eyes usually closed, it would remain motionless save for a slow movement of its pectoral fins forward and back, much like an opera singer swinging his arms," said Paul, conjuring a scene as extraordinary as the music.

Zoologists Roger and Katy Payne discovered that "humpbacks are inveterate composers constantly tinkering with their songs," as Roger wrote in a NATIONAL GEOGRAPHIC report. Although the changes are fairly subtle at the end of one season, the new phrases accumulate, and after a few years the songs have become significantly different.

Everything about these elusive, enigmatic beings inspires awe—their size and grace, their baffling, beautiful songs, and their improbable

existence as intelligent, affectionate mammals utterly at home in the sea. Surely that is why even fleeting encounters with them are so exhilarating and why thousands of people embark on whale-watching tours.

"The bad news is that heavy boat traffic may be impacting the whales," says Professor Joseph R. Mobley of the University of Hawaii, co-author of a survey of whale populations that revealed a threefold increase in the number of humpbacks in waters around Niihau, a little-traveled area. Some scientists are concerned that human activity may be pushing whales into deeper waters, which are not as well suited to calving.

Joe is keeping his conclusions tentative because the impact of boats on whales is hard to prove. "We've only been monitoring the population about 15 years," he told me. "And the shift to Niihau may be part of a normal cycle of movement."

A conservationist who took a stronger stand told me that, for animals with hearing as sensitive as the humpbacks', the boat traffic must be like having someone with a weed whacker following them all day. Concern about human disturbance led to the establishment of the Hawaiian Islands Humpback Whale National Marine Sanctuary in November 1992.

The waters off Lanai's south and southwest coasts harbor some of Hawaii's most pristine coral reefs, home to creatures as cryptic and magical as the humpbacks. Staring down through my snorkel mask at those undersea landscapes pulsing with life was like being suspended above a giant kaleidoscope.

In the course of a few minutes in the water around Po'opo'o Island, I saw an amazing array of fish. A school of Moorish idols—black-white-and-yellow, trailing a white plume from their dorsal fins—swam out of the recesses of a lava canyon. Silvery convict tangs moved in a much larger school, spilling over a crag of dark lava like a shower of crystal. A yellow tang flashed by, its color like a stab of light. Iridescent blue-green parrotfish hovered next to patches of cauliflower coral. I could hear crackling as they scraped algae from the coral and crunched them with teeth fused into a parrotlike beak. The mouths of the butterflyfish were elongated into a pout, and their bodies, so slender they seemed like paper cutouts, were marked with a combination of stripes, streaks, dots, or large eyespots.

There were many more species, and Ann Fielding seemed able to identify them all. A lively, youthful woman, Ann is a zoologist and an enthusiastic diver whose books and guided snorkel trips have introduced many people to Hawaii's underwater world. Departing once again from Mānele harbor, we were bound for some of Lanai's best snorkeling spots.

Kicking lazily with fins on my feet *(Continued on page 106)*

Coconut palms etch a twilight sky on Molokai. The stately trees, part of Kapuāiwa Grove, were planted in the mid-1800s by King Kamehameha V.

FOLLOWING PAGES: A humpback whale keeps company with her calf along Whale Highway—the shallow Auau Channel between Lanai and Maui.

FLIP NICKLIN / MINDEN PICTURES

A harlequin shrimp dines on a favorite delicacy—a red sea star. Extravagant

DAVID DOUBILET

colors of the reef may help creatures find mates—and avoid competitors—scientists believe.

Denizens of the deep patrol the reefs and rocks of the Hawaiian archipelago. A sponge crab, rarely seen outside the lava tubes where it lives, eyes photographer Doubilet "with a forlorn, pinched look." An anthius (opposite) glimmers in deep waters off Niihau. Some 450 fish species inhabit Hawaiian waters, about a quarter of them unique to the islands.

FOLLOWING PAGES: *An oceanic whitetip shark, a blue-water species, cruises off the island of Hawaii. Because the islands are oceanic, deep waters exist only a few miles offshore. Some ancient Hawaiians revered sharks as guardian spirits—*'aumakua*—and their meat was spurned by many clans as taboo.*

DAVID DOUBILET (ABOVE, OPPOSITE, AND FOLLOWING PAGES)

and floating above a polychrome wonderland, I could easily lose track of time. The clarity of the water also misled me: Each time I tried to dive down to a clump of coral, I found that it was farther away than it seemed. I had hoped to see the reef triggerfish, a colorful, solitary species that is the state fish of Hawaii, locally called *humuhumu-nukunuku-a-pua'a,* a name that has the distinction of being one of the longest words in Webster's unabridged dictionary. I asked Ann about the abundant speckled, bright yellow fish marked with a single black, vertical stripe across its head and eyes. It was the millet-seed butterflyfish, found only in Hawaii.

"It's like a village down there, with different neighborhoods. The Achilles surgeonfish like the surge areas. The blue-striped butterflies keep to the sandy bottoms near rocky outcrops. Cleaner wrasses set up service stations where they pick off the parasites plaguing their clients. Fish arrive at these spots and wait their turn to be cleaned. About 25 percent of the species of reef and shore fish and 20 percent of the mollusks and sea stars

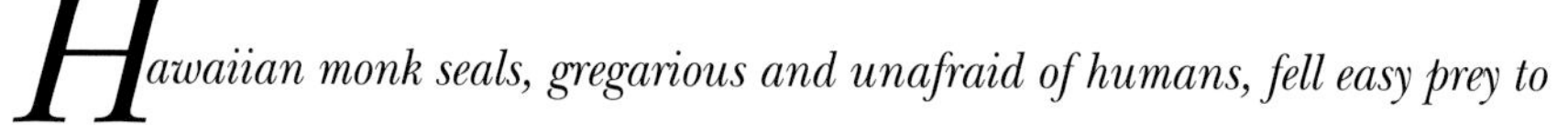

Hawaiian monk seals, gregarious and unafraid of humans, fell easy prey to

are found nowhere else in the world," said Ann, as we rounded Palaoa Point. "All shore fish and marine life had to come to these islands on currents across the barrier of open ocean that isolates Hawaii. Only a limited number of organisms made it."

Hawaii's sea creatures made the journey in their larval form, a stage in which they are buoyant and passive enough to be carried great distances by ocean currents. Those species with a long larval life were the most successful castaways. Surgeonfish, which take two and a half months to metamorphose into adults, are well represented in Hawaii. In contrast, groupers mature in 23 days—not enough time to drift to these islands.

The process was gradual, with the islands strewn across the western and central Pacific acting as stepping-stones.

Take the corals: In many species the larva settles down just days after the egg is fertilized. For the rest of its life it lives as a pinhead-size polyp ensconced in a limestone container of its own making. Just 42 out of

19th-century sealers. Today these endangered animals are under intensive protection.

BILL CURTSINGER

several hundred species of coral in the Pacific made the long journey to Hawaii. In many cases, the rocks and reefs have been colonized not by corals but by the coralline algae, which also manufacture calcium carbonate.

Along the barren cliffs beyond Kaunolū Bay we dropped anchor and slipped into the water again at Shark Fin Rock, a pinnacle rising above the surface. It is part of a ridge running perpendicular to the coast. Near shore, the surging waves turned light green as they curled over exposed lava platforms, spilling in miniature cascades down the shiny black rock. We were well beyond the surf, however, and merely bobbed in the deep blue swells.

Underwater, the topography is dominated by prominent lava formations, which often generate a lot of currents. The upwelling around these vertical walls stirs up nutrients, attracting plankton and the many fish that feed on them. Wrasses in neon hues and elaborate markings cruised alongside a variety of surgeonfish, named for the one or more lancelike spines that grow at the base of the tail. In this family I could easily identify the Achilles tang with its Halloween colors and the bluespine unicornfish with a horn on its forehead.

Scientists have a theory to explain the extravaganza of color on the reef. "In the crowded population, markings help a fish recognize mating partners as well as its competitors for food," said Ann. She also pointed out that many of the brightest fish have dark, slanted bars that break up their outline against the crazy-quilt pattern of the reef—a form of camouflage called disruptive coloration.

Ann dived down to a clump of cauliflower coral and pointed to a slate pencil sea urchin armored with broad, blunt, orange-red spines. Though these urchins are rare elsewhere, they are abundant in the islands. Eels have also done well, for they did not have to compete for prey with snappers and groupers, which are poorly represented in these waters.

Eels may now have lost this edge. In the 1950s the state Department of Land and Natural Resources tampered with the natural ecosystem: Biologists introduced a grouper and three South Pacific species of coral-reef snappers. The blue-striped fish known by its Tahitian name *ta'ape* is thriving, and such native predators as eels and goatfish are confronted with new, aggressive competition that threatens to disrupt the established balance.

Unlike snorkelers, scuba divers are equipped to explore Lanai's huge underwater grottoes and lava tubes, and they can also swim down to the mollusks, crustaceans, and myriad other invertebrates that inhabit the depths. There, sponges encrust rocks like splotches of enamel paint. Feeding on them are nudibranchs, or sea slugs, with names like Spanish dancer and gold lace. They move slowly through the water, waving feathery gills. Improbable creatures such as featherduster and Christmas tree worms burrow into the coral and flutter frilled tentacles to capture plankton for food.

We traveled along the west coast as far as Kaumalapau Harbor. Blasted out of rock in the 1920s, it provided a port for barges shipping pineapples to the cannery in Honolulu when the island was still in the fruit business. The harbor was deserted that day except for a pod of three Pacific bottle-nosed dolphins that sped past us, as if hurrying to an appointment.

For Ann the undersea panorama is endlessly fascinating. Clive Cabiles, an avid spear fisherman in his early 30s, has another mission when he swims in Lanai's waters—food. His usual catch consists of six- or seven-pound parrotfish and tang, but he proudly boasts of a 72-pound jack he once bagged with his homemade spear gun.

One of his favorite haunts is Shipwreck Beach, an eight-mile stretch of sand along Lanai's northeast coast. It has earned its name several times over the years—both from ships that ran aground on the reef and from others that were deliberately towed there and abandoned.

"Every hole in the offshore reef is like my refrigerator," says Clive, confident he knows where spiny lobsters and local fish hang out.

Like most of Lanai's residents, Clive came from the Philippines.

"My father worked his buns off in the pineapple fields and lived on salted fish to save money to bring his family here," he said, as we drove from the cool heights of Lanai City down to the shore, where the pavement ends. Clive turned north on the ribbon of dirt road paralleling the beach. Most of the way it passed through a corridor of scrubby Chilean mesquite—*kiawe*—that walls the succession of beaches along this uninhabited coast.

"I started working in the fields as a picker when I was 14. It was a summer job for a lot of kids in high school. We wore long sleeves and pants, heavy gloves, and bandannas around our faces to keep from being scratched by the prickly fruit and sharp leaves. It was too hot, too dusty, and too hard on the feet and back, so when I graduated I left for the mainland."

Like a lot of young people who have returned to Lanai to work at the new hotels, Clive likes being back on Lanai. He has friends and relatives everywhere, and only a handful of local people fish the miles of shoreline.

Our destination was a rambling shack on the southern end of Shipwreck Beach, where aunts, cousins, in-laws, and friends of the Cabiles family gather almost every weekend.

One of the clan was grilling an octopus he had just caught.

"You can recognize its den by the piles of shells stacked around the entrance," said Clive. "They're left over from its lunches. You tickle the octopus with this stick"—a three-prong rod—"and it will come out of its hole. You just catch it or spear it."

He concedes that sometimes there's a little more to it.

"Once I made the mistake of grabbing an especially big one right after I shot it. Its arms were still strong, and it was pulling my snorkel off with one arm and trying to choke me with another two. I managed to swim to shore with it still writhing on my back."

Spiny lobsters, which gourmets consider a real delicacy, also inhabit holes in the reef, and Clive and his uncle Bruno Amby like to hunt them at night, when they are active. With an underwater light it's easy to spot their long, waving antennae. "But you have to watch out for eels, because they hide in the same places."

Clive admits it's scary when an eel brushes by in the darkness. But like most of the local people, he showed little concern about sharks. If he's near a turtle in deep water, however, he moves away. "Sharks eat turtles.

Some surfers think that's why they get in trouble, because they look like turtles on their boards." According to a tally by a National Marine Fisheries Service scientist, there were 105 presumed shark incidents in Hawaiian waters between 1779 and 1993; 17 were witnessed attacks that led to deaths.

That night, when Clive went fishing for spiny lobsters with missionary doctor Robert Smith, the problem was neither eels nor sharks. It was the current and the rough water whipped to a froth by a strong wind.

Robert returned utterly exhausted by an hour-long struggle in the water. "In some places I was kicking hard and not getting anywhere. I'd be in the same spot looking at the same little red fish. Other times I had to hang on to rocks to keep from being swept away. Wherever I could, I poled myself along with my spear. All the while I was getting hit with the waves."

Clive was not happy either; his catch was only two spiny lobsters.

Trade winds blowing at 25 to 30 knots persisted the next day and roiled the water into a murky chop. Clive's father had been studying the water, watching for fish in the curl of the waves, and decided it was not a good day. Two other fishermen took up positions down the beach and tried surf casting anyway. A short walk beyond them and children splashing in the surf led me to miles of shore with no one on it.

Beach morning glory trailed purple flowers across the gray sand, and beach naupaka grew in low green patches on the dunes. But the coast was kiawe country, and the thorny branches with ferny leaves formed thickets that leaned away from the trade winds. Spurs of lava divided the strand into segments and provided places to sit. Much driftwood had been cast ashore by the strong currents. There was a somber loveliness to the scene, underscored by the hulk of an abandoned barge listing woefully on the reef.

On the lee side of the island, away from the stiff trades, a soft breeze barely stirred the palms of Hulopo'e Beach Park, a paragon of the South Seas paradise of everyone's dream. Little waves lapped at the wide crescent of white sand. Beyond the surf, which gave the children on boogie boards a gentle ride, the turquoise waters of Hulopo'e Bay beckoned. The best swimming area on Lanai, it is part of the Mānele-Hulopo'e Marine Life Conservation District, which protects the bay from pollution, the fish from depletion, and the reefs from damage by divers and boats' anchors.

Spinner dolphins regularly frolic in the bay, springing out of the water with a characteristic whirl. It's against the law to approach these small, delightful creatures, but what can one do if they swim near? There's no telling why they did not come to Hulopo'e that day—which gives me another reason to return to the special enchantment of Lanai's shores.

Swift, trim, and frolicsome, spinner dolphins traveling in a pod engage in sexual play near barren Lehua rock off Niihau.

FOLLOWING PAGES: A Hawaiian turkeyfish gazes at its reflection in pools of air bubbles trapped on the ceiling of a lava tube. This endemic fish is the most venomous scorpionfish in Hawaiian waters.

DAVID DOUBILET (OPPOSITE AND FOLLOWING PAGES)

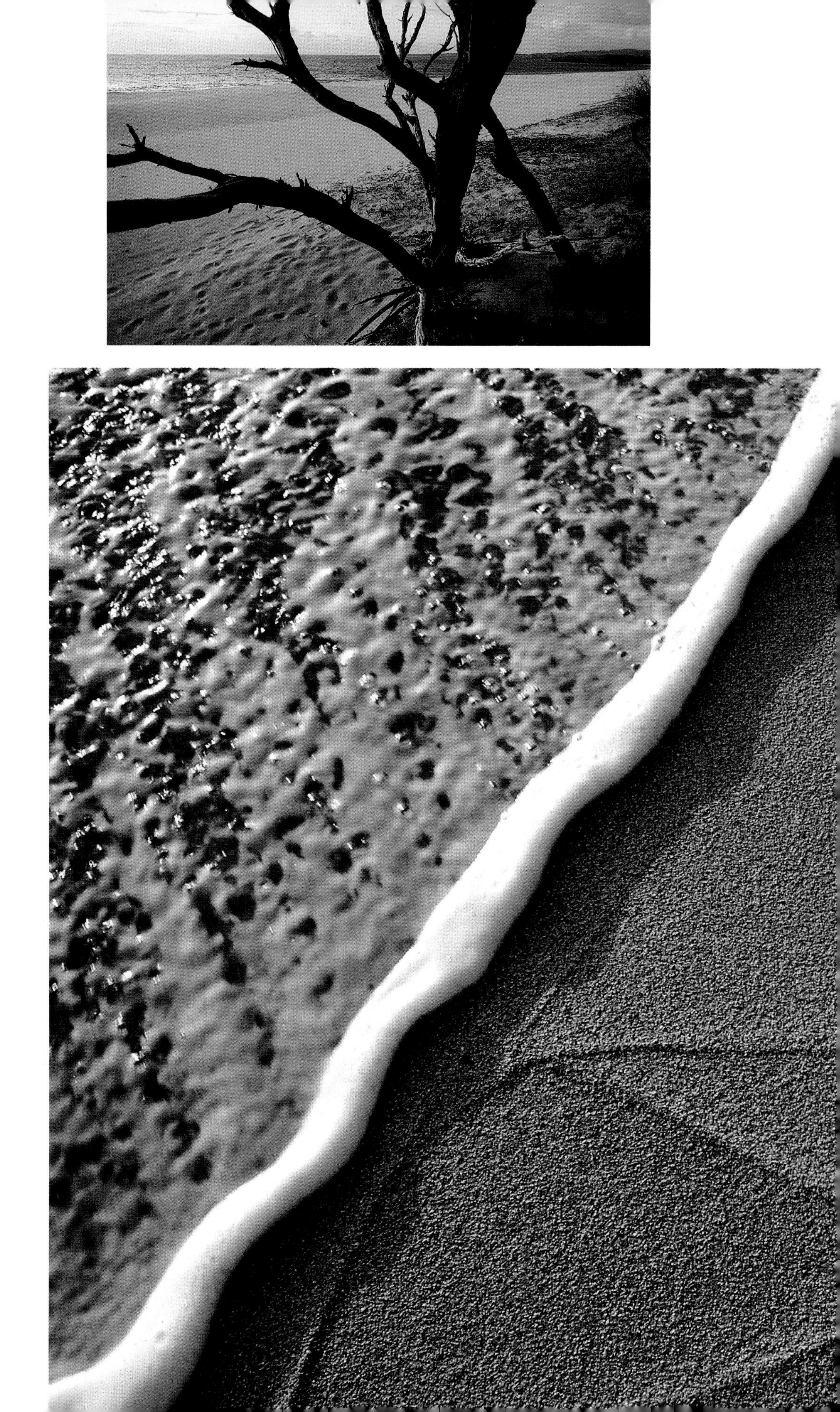

Foaming ripples form overlapping shingle patterns on the sands of Pāpōhaku Beach. The three-mile strand (opposite), located on the western side of Molokai, is regarded as Hawaii's longest white-sand beach. Barges have transported some of its sands to improve the beach at Waikiki in Honolulu.

FOLLOWING PAGES: Only nature's footprints—wind-formed ripples and the swirls of a breeze-blown twig—blemish Molokai's remote Mo'omomi Beach.

SEA CLIFFS AND SECLUDED

We rocked on the swells, waiting. Before us, breakers rolled across the reef, menacing our exit from Halawa Bay. Glenn Davis, who, with his curly hair and beard might have been cast by Hollywood for the role of Polynesian voyager, was staring ahead, keeping track of the waves. At Halawa they usually come in a series of seven, he said, and a boat has to start moving in the pause between sets to make it out to the deep waters along Molokai's north shore.

"Now!" Glenn shouted, gunning the motor and warning me to hang on. With a burst from the twin outboard motors we blasted through the steep, breaking waves. The 18-foot boat bounced hard again and again. Waves slammed against the hull. Their foaming crests smacked the windshield, splashing us with spray.

"Once you begin, you're committed. You don't stop or slow down, no matter what's coming at you. Even if waves are breaking inside the boat, it's safer to punch through," said Glenn, once we were outside the bay. "Coming out of Halawa is always tricky and rough. When a boat is surfing down the back of a wave, you'll lose control unless you keep the nose up."

It was somewhat easier going as we slowed down and plowed west along the coast, passing towering cliffs that plunged straight into the sea. On their slopes, wind-ruffled waterfalls trailed streamers of mist.

Though it was a mild summer morning, the water was a chaos of cresting swells. No islands or reefs buffer this windward shore from waves that sweep across thousands of miles of open ocean and slam into the volcanic walls. The backwash churns the sea with reflected waves. Agitating the mix are the trade winds, a constant onslaught blowing at 10 to 25 knots. These stiff winds also strike the cliffs and ricochet back onto the ocean, bringing yet another chop to what is called washing-machine water. A local woman told me that in six years she had seen it glass-flat here just twice.

In summer, skilled mariners can maneuver through this boisterous sea. But in winter, when 30-foot swells charge down from the stormy North Pacific and explode on shore, local traffic comes to a halt. From November to May, the 14 miles between the Halawa Valley and the Kalaupapa Peninsula are virtually cut off from the rest of Molokai and the world. And at any time of year, it is the most isolated shoreline in all of Hawaii.

The rest of the 40 or so miles of the windward coast is somewhat more accessible. Visitors can reach the Halawa Valley on the east end by car. In the west, a dirt road leads to the Mo'omomi Dunes. The road, however, is part of the Home Lands set aside for lease to native Hawaiians, and some locals want to limit public use. The Kalaupapa Peninsula, site of a famous leprosy settlement that is now a national historical park, receives

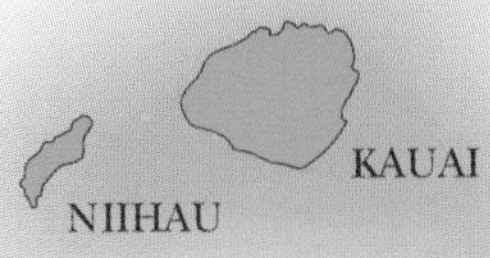

VALLEYS

regular plane service. There is also a steep trail that goes from topside to the settlement.

My odyssey to windward Molokai began with the jolting voyage to the remote reaches west of Halawa. On the advice of Glenn I wore a bathing suit—because I would have to swim ashore—and *tabi,* split-toed, felt-soled socks of Japanese origin that provide traction when clambering on wet, slippery rocks. I would camp at Wailau Valley and then spend a few days at Hā'upu Bay with the only people that now live year-round on this stretch of coast.

The Guinness Book of Records states that "the highest sea cliffs...in the world are those on the north coast of East Molokai...which descend 3,300 feet to the sea at an average gradient of more than 55°." Reading the entry did not prepare me for the grand spectacle of this rock-bound shore.

There was a massive dignity to the ramparts rising like a bastion from the infinity of the ocean. Vegetation mellowed the volcanic walls, but the greenery did not blur the sheer drops that gave the shoreline a citadel look. There were ferns and mosses, but the hala, or pandanus tree, was the predominant plant. Propped on aerial roots, halas found footholds on the tiniest ledges and grew so snug against the curve of the cliffs that the rosettes of long leaves seemed splayed against the rock. Wherever there was a strip of shore between the cliffs and the sea, the trees multiplied into thickets, a reminder that this was the tropics.

More than the palm or any other plant, the hala, with its sword-shaped leaves fanning out from the tips of bare branches, evokes for me the wet, wild coasts of Hawaii. For the ancient Hawaiians, who wove the foliage into mats, baskets, and sails and utilized virtually every part of the tree, the hala was vital to their lives.

The terrain was heavily furrowed by ephemeral streams that run after a heavy rain. More permanent watercourses had carved four valleys along the north shore beyond Halawa. As we neared the shallow Pāpalaua Valley, I saw the silver shimmer of a slender waterfall, the first of many visible from the boat. None were thundering torrents. Some dropped in a single gleaming white plume; others stair-stepped down, leaping, splashing, and frothing from ledge to ledge. They brought to the landscape a sparkling exuberance as joyful as birdsong.

FOLLOWING PAGES: Highest sea cliffs in the world, Molokai's north coast pali rise in places more than 3,000 feet above inky Pacific depths. During part of the year, rough seas limit access to the remote region.

Rounding Lēpau Point, we came upon the huge green amphitheater of Wailau, one of the largest valleys on Molokai. It stretched inland four miles, ending in a mountain rising sharply to almost 5,000 feet. Majestic, it stood like some grand monument set down upon the verdant land.

In the lee of the headland were calmer waters, where visitors to the valley anchor their boats and swim the short distance to the boulder beach. Glenn loaded my gear onto a raft improvised from an inner tube fastened to a square board. Glenn's brother Theodore, called Teddy Bear, swam it ashore. A friend's fox terrier rode solemnly on the wobbling rubber rim with the panache of an admiral.

A dozen youngsters were frolicking in the jade-green water. They were the nieces, nephews, cousins, son, and friends of Joe and Sharleen Kalima, who had set up camp on the beach for the summer. Beyond the shore and the mouth of Wailau Stream, the broad, cliff-girt valley was a luxuriant blur except for the coconut palms and leafy banana trees that rimmed the beach. On the slopes the candlenut trees, called kukui, traced a pale green calligraphy against the darker green of the forest.

Joe, a fisherman from Kaunakakai, the island's small main town, and his wife, Sharleen, had rigged a cookhouse-dining room and dormitory of bamboo poles lashed together with strips of inner tube. Plastic tarps covered the two large frame structures—one furnished with long tables, the other with mattresses lined up on platforms. There was always a place for members of the Kalima extended family and their friends, who would come and go all summer.

Shirts, shorts, and towels were drying on a clothesline strung between the two open-sided pavilions. Chicken adobo, a Philippine-style stew made with vinegar, bay leaves, black pepper, and soy sauce, was simmering in a big black kettle on a propane stove in the rear of the kitchen. Also in the back were tub-size coolers crammed with cans of soda and beer.

When I first met Sharleen, she was slicing a green coconut for two slender teenagers with long, glossy hair. Sharleen's hair had never been cut, and when she untied it in the evenings it hung down to her hips. At those times she looked like one of the solemn, stately women in Paul Gauguin's South Seas paintings.

Joe, who is more gregarious than Sharleen, is three-quarters Hawaiian and one-quarter Japanese, but, like so many of mixed ancestry, he takes particular pride in his Polynesian roots. He was filleting *akule,* or mackerel, that he had just caught from the shore with a round, weighted net. It is flung with both hands, somewhat like a Frisbee. It is difficult to do correctly. "If you throw it too high, it floats down too slow, and the fish see it coming and escape. If you throw it too low, you don't get the good spread. But if you work it right, you can catch a whole bunch of fish—like mullet, mackerel, and parrotfish, the kind that hang out close to shore," said Joe.

He handed me a large, shiny ti leaf, saying, "You can hush the flies away while you ask all those questions. We still believe that fish have ears, so we never announce we're going fishing. Instead we say we are going *'auwana,* which means just roaming around the water to see what happens."

Like many people born on Molokai, Joe has ties to Wailau Valley, which was inhabited year-round as late as the 1930s. There were frame houses along the beach, and the whole four-mile length of the valley was under cultivation, with rows of terraces planted with taro and sweet potatoes. Joe's father carried mail into the valley, regularly walking into Wailau from the south shore on a seven-mile trail. Today the trail is barely discernible and rarely used. It's so steep that the occasional hikers pick their way along, hanging onto branches and using tree roots as ladder rungs.

"The taro and houses are all gone," said Joe. "Some hippies came in the seventies and planted bamboo and grew *paka lōlō*—marijuana—back in the woods. They're also gone now, but somehow the valley remains the same. For us, Wailau is this special place where we can still find the Hawaii that used to be."

Old-timer Rachel Naki remembers Wailau when "people raised up cows and pigs" and regularly left offerings to Kauhuhu, the shark god. "Those days very strict. You cannot dance the hula. If you sing hula song you gonna get a hundred sticks on your backside."

Born in 1905, Rachel reminisced about her childhood in the valley while she was hoeing in her front yard. "It was beautiful when you could see only taro. Now no more taro patches, only weeds," she said, shaking her head in dismay.

"When we cooked taro, all the aunts and uncles coming with their poi boards and stones to help pound poi. In those days the machine was your hand. Now, people take their own food to Wailau," Rachel told me, chuckling at the oddity with a broad, toothless smile.

"OK. I'm going to turn my hand down," she said, resuming hoeing.

For Rachel, Wailau is "all different today."

Yet the valley's soul remains Hawaiian. For Joe Kalima and others who speak of the north shore with such nostalgia, a visit to Wailau returns them to the idealized virtues of earlier times, when people enjoyed a kinship with the community and lived close to the land.

Though people do bring in some provisions, locals regularly supplement their supplies in the still bountiful valley. People hike up the river and its tributaries to collect *hīhīwai,* a freshwater snail that has become a rare treat. It lives in unspoiled streams that are still flowing free.

There are also feasts of gobies, prawns, and shrimp to be found in the remote streambeds. And beyond the shelter of Lēpau Point, the wave-battered boulders on Wailau's mile-long beach are speckled with the *'opihi,* a species of limpet in conical shells.

Joe and his family know where to go for mountain apples, mangoes, guavas, and bananas. From time to time someone will hike into the mountains and shoot an axis deer, a species imported into the island in the 1860s, and the meat will be shared with friends and neighbors.

The summer days, scented with the honey-sweet perfume of ginger blossoms, go by as softly as the mist drifting down from the high ridges. People bathe in the river, green with the reflection of the trees arching over the water, and stroll along a stretch of black sand, wet and gleaming in the pearly twilight. And when darkness *(Continued on page 130)*

Sheltering ramparts of Molokai's north coast dwarf the home of Joyce Kainoa and Mike Donleavey at remote Keavanui on Hā'upu Bay. In 1978, "Cultural clashes—Western versus Hawaiian—and a search for an alternative life-style" brought Joyce, a native Hawaiian, to a rocky bluff accessible only by boat, helicopter, or an 11-hour hike over rugged terrain. There she and Mike built their home, with terraced taro patches and gardens. To rear her family in the cultural ways of her ancestors, she taught her children "their Bible lessons, respect for their cultural identity and family, stewardship of natural resources for future generations, and how to live in harmony first with nature—then with man." Above, her son, Sammy, now grown, stands at road's end with his wife, Casey, and their son.

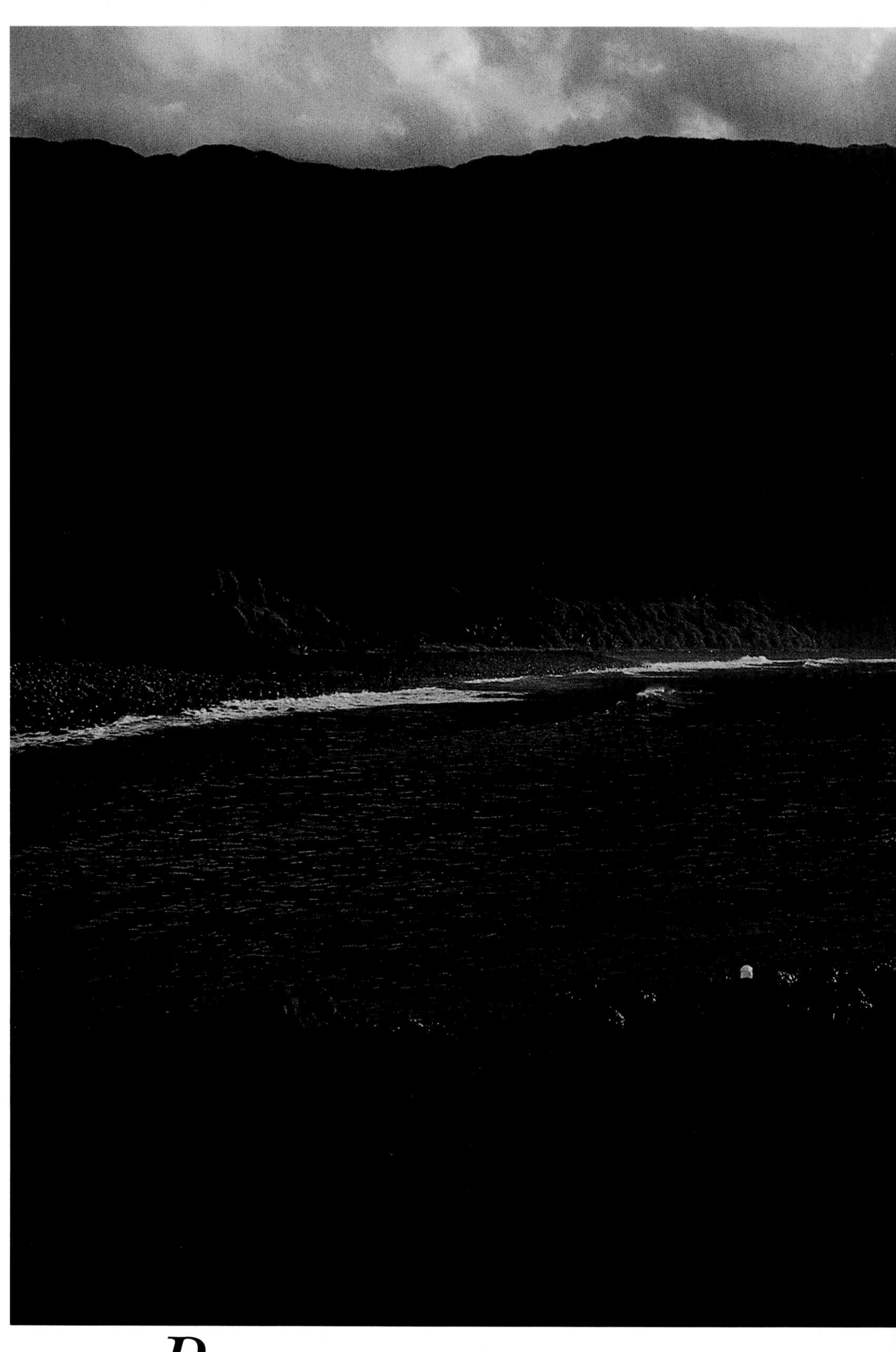

Back for more, a young swimmer scales a rocky outcrop to plunge again into

the sea at Molokai's Wailau Valley, where she camped during the summer.

With a smile as bright as sunshine, a young native Hawaiian emerges from the surf at Wailau Valley. Other bathers at Halawa Bay frolic under a thundering waterfall, in the tradition of ancestors who fished and played at water's edge. "A water of magic power—The water of life! O give us this life!" goes a sacred chant to Kāne, ancient Hawaiian god of water.

falls and hands reach for ukuleles and guitars, the nights ring with music and laughter.

Isolation is part of Wailau's allure, and many local people are concerned that an onslaught of visitors will destroy its special character. Wailau is cherished as a place to get away from it all, even though the rest of Molokai moves to its own slow drumbeat and retains a balmy, small-town air. There's only one large resort on the island, and, despite pressure from developers, the Molokai community is intent on controlling the future growth of the resort industry.

"Other islands have put too many eggs in the tourism basket," said Glenn Teves, a county agent with the University of Hawaii Cooperative Extension Service. On Molokai, which has a population of only 6,000, visitors "can really have an impact on traffic, parking spaces in Kaunakakai, and food on the market shelves," says Glenn. Articulate and outspoken, Glenn, like many other native Hawaiians I met, was reserved at first, waiting, I think, for some gesture of real interest before relaxing.

Water is the key to development on Molokai, because condos and golf courses have an insatiable thirst, and proposed projects are on the arid western side of the island. People of 50 percent Hawaiian ancestry, who are entitled to 40 acres of land under a federal homestead program, also want water.

"In many places on the other islands developers have negotiated directly with the state government, making back-room deals by lobbying state and county bureaucrats for permits and water rights. That's harder to do on Molokai, where the community is determined to control its destiny. We have overflow crowds attending public hearings," Glenn had told me, as we talked in his office in Hoʻolehua, a community of about 500 residents. "When it comes to water, the resource is not infinite, and the needs of native Hawaiian homesteaders and farmers come first," insists Glenn.

Any major change in consumption would mean tapping into streams on the north shore and tunneling the water through the mountains. Prime candidates are the streams in Wailau or Pelekunu, a lush valley purchased by the Nature Conservancy to protect its endangered ecosystem.

Only 10 percent of Hawaii's 300 year-round streams remain in a natural state. A few of them are on Molokai, and, says Glenn, the community doesn't want to suck these last unspoiled rivers dry for golf courses.

"We have to arrive at a better balance between development and the protection of our last wildlife areas. We don't measure success by a bank account. We admire generosity and hospitality. People here look at the islanders as one extended family, and we watch out for each other. Molokai is the only island that doesn't have youth gangs, because kids can get a spanking not only from parents but also from all their aunties and uncles."

Many people on Molokai still meet their needs in part by subsistence hunting, fishing, and gathering seaweed and other plants. Some hunters see a threat to their life-style in hunting regulations and in removing pigs, goats, and deer from Kamakou and Pelekunu, Nature Conservancy preserves on the island. Like the state and the National Park Service, the Conservancy regulates hunting and also has a policy of removing non-native wildlife from the most pristine forests, using snares or aerial shooting for animal control.

"As a hunter I have a feeling for where the pigs are. I don't want anyone telling where I can go, and in certain areas my dogs may get caught in their snares," grumbles hunter Joseph Mawae. Glenn says, "The issue for these Hawaiians is asserting native and traditional gathering rights."

On the other hand, says Alan Holt, director of science and stewardship for the Nature Conservancy, the survival of plants and animals found nowhere else in the world is at stake. "We think of snaring as a last-ditch resort, which has in fact reduced damage levels," asserts Alan. "There is a legitimate place for hunting, but there is also a serious need to protect the remote areas. If we can't control pigs, we can't save the forest."

Perhaps no one on Molokai cares more about life-style than Joyce Kainoa and her partner, Mike Donleavey. They live year-round at Keavanui on Hā'upu Bay. It is five miles and a dozen or so waterfalls west of Wailau, separated from Pelekunu Valley by a high ridge. Self-reliant and resourceful, Joyce and Mike meet their basic needs in their hard-earned utopia much as Joyce's Hawaiian forbears did.

They came in September 1978 with five of her children, aged 5 to 11. Winter was approaching, so they had to unload about 10,000 pounds of goods in a hurry; soon 30-footers would be breaking on the beach.

In those days the rain forest began just beyond the fringe of boulders at the water's edge, and they had to cut their way inland. They hacked out trails and switchbacks up to their homesite. They cleared the slopes and learned how to make the land productive. With Mike's engineering skills they built a gravity-flow irrigation system and transported water from the river in pipes to turn a Pelton wheel, which generates electricity.

"We brought cement with us, but the mortar came from the next valley to the east, a mile away. All of us packed the sand and gravel in. We did it just three times a week, so the kids wouldn't rebel," said Joyce, as we sat at sunset in the large cookhouse with its blue tile floor and lovely stone fireplace. Looking across the manicured lawn and garden, I could see a panorama of cliffs jutting into the sea 250 feet below.

"To be realistic, I knew I could never live in the real ancient Hawaiian way. I could never cope with it. But I have tried to give my kids some sense of what it means to be Hawaiian. I wanted to teach them how to live off the land and the ocean, so they could always feed themselves. I taught them that we are custodians of the earth, and we have a responsibility to keep it for the next generation. You take only as much as you need to put food on the table.

"I wanted them to be patient and humble before nature. For example, sometimes we have to accept the fact that we can't go to Kaunakakai because the ocean is too rough. Who are you going to argue with? Not with God, that's for sure. As a Hawaiian, I wanted them to be proud of what they are and where they come from. We've listened too long to another culture telling us we're lazy and good-for-nothing. So many Hawaiians are poor and poorly educated. So many of our young people are delinquents and in jail because they've lost their identity and can't handle living in a dual culture. We were discouraged from using our Hawaiian language. We were not taught our history. Our values were undermined. We lost our land. We lost touch with our roots. We became foreigners in our own islands."

Joyce has become a spokeswoman for her people, and from time to time she returns to the outside world to campaign for Hawaiian rights.

A vigorous, handsome woman in her 40s, she became aware of her Hawaiian heritage in the mid-1970s during an emotional campaign to stop the shelling of Kahoolawe. The island, visible from the south coast of Maui, had been used as an artillery range by the U. S. Navy since World War II.

Gathering his net on Kawākiu Nui Bay, Kimo Naki uses skills learned from

"The bombardment was desecrating land where Hawaiians had lived in ancient times and was destroying archaeological sites and *heiau,*" said Joyce. Heiau are places of worship, ranging from upright stones to massive temple platforms. "The Protect Kahoolawe movement was a terrific catalyst. It opened the gates to the Hawaiian renaissance. We learned to speak up. It gave us confidence," Joyce said. "My own reawakening began in jail, waiting for my trial on charges of trespassing on Kahoolawe. Many of us occupied the island at different times," she said, with a proud smile.

"There were books in the jail library. For the first time I learned about the overthrow of Queen Liliuokalani in 1893 by American sugar

elders. Circular throw nets were brought to Hawaii by the Japanese a century ago.

planters and businessmen, who were backed by the U. S. Marines. It was engineered by interests that wanted the Kingdom of Hawaii annexed to the United States so Hawaiian sugar could enter the protected American market duty free. I was never taught anything about all this in school."

For the 140,000 people who claim 50 percent Hawaiian blood—about 12 percent of the population—the newfound pride has become firmly entrenched. On the heels of this cultural resurgence, there has been a steady growth of interest in sovereignty, with a variety of political groups seeking some measure of self-government or even independence.

Next morning a gray mist descended from low clouds. Though much of the world was a ghostly blur, there was a single band of clarity to the west. It brought into focus the Kalaupapa Peninsula, formed by an eruption that sent lava flowing against the bluffs. It had created a finger of land projecting from the cliffs that lay on the pewter sea, long and dark, like the pall of anguish cast upon the leprosy patients once exiled there.

A few days later I hiked the 2.4-mile trail that spirals down 26 switchbacks to the peninsula, which has become a national park dedicated to a remarkable chapter of Hawaiian history.

Leprosy, like measles and the flu, did not exist on the islands before the coming of Europeans and Asians. By 1860, leprosy was rampant among the Hawaiians, who had little immunity to outside diseases. To halt the epidemic, King Kamehameha V chose the Kalaupapa Peninsula, hemmed in between the cliffs and the pounding surf, to be a leprosy settlement.

For decades, from the time the first patients were shipped to the peninsula in 1866, Kalaupapa was a place shrouded in dread and fear. For the Hawaiians, leprosy was a catastrophe, not only because it was maiming and disfiguring, but also because it wrenched families apart. Hawaiians called it "the separating sickness." For most victims, until the 1960s when doctors in Hawaii started using drugs to arrest the disease and render it noncontagious, Kalaupapa was a place of no return.

"My father was banished here when I was nine years old," recalled Richard Marks, a husky 61-year-old who had been sentenced to the settlement in 1956. "My baby sister was only five when they took her away and put her in the home for girls here. Like anyone with the disease in the immediate family, I had to go for a checkup every month. If you didn't show up, the cops would come for you."

Now Richard runs one of the tour companies that offers the public access to the Kalaupapa National Historical Park, established in 1980. To protect the privacy of the 80 patients still living there, it is a restricted area; visitors must have a permit and a guide.

As we drove through the tidy village of small cottages, churches, library, bar, infirmary, and state-run general store, I learned that the average age of the remaining patients was 70. They all had been residents at least 30 years—and some more than 50. Since 1969 they have been free to leave. Most have stayed on.

"Where can we go? For years official policy scared the hell out of everybody about having us around," observed Richard dryly. "My brother left three different times. Then a social worker would go to his boss and announce, 'This guy has leprosy. Don't give him difficult jobs.' Each time, my brother got so damned discouraged he ended up back here. It wasn't bad enough that you got sick. They had to make you feel ashamed for it.

"But you can't blame the public; they were never taught any better. Now they come up with this nonsense of calling it Hansen's disease"—for the Norwegian scientist who discovered the leprosy bacillus in 1873. "I don't think you change anything by changing the name. Instead, people need to know the facts. It is far less contagious than most people think. Only 5 percent of the world's population is even susceptible to it. Now with modern drugs even the worst cases soon become noninfectious."

We left the village of Kalaupapa and drove along a broad gravel road under a leafy tunnel of Java plum trees to the St. Philomena Church. Nothing else is left of the first settlement on the east side of the peninsula, which was called Kalawao. Nothing except the fame of Father Damien, the roughhewn Belgian priest, born Joseph DeVeuster, who devoted himself to Hawaii's forsaken and forgotten outcasts.

In the seven years before Damien arrived in 1873, Kalawao was a living nightmare, a lawless lazaretto of debauchery, neglected by the world.

"Damien worked no miracles, cured no patients. He just showed them that somebody cared," said Richard, as we entered the restored church. "He came to build a church but refused to go back. In one of his letters Damien wrote, 'I feel I have found my true calling. Here I walk a path and move a stone, and I help someone.'"

Richard explained: "To understand what he meant, you've got to realize the lepers had no shoes and were often walking along in six inches of mud. If they accidentally kicked a rock, they could damage a toe and develop gangrene." For the community, which at times had a population of a thousand or more, Father Damien did more than move stones. He planted hundreds of fruit trees; he built a hospital, housing, and a water system; he organized games and consoled the dying; he badgered authorities into providing cement, lumber and clothing, and better food.

One of many famous visitors here was Robert Louis Stevenson, who came in 1889. In a letter from Hawaii, he wrote that "the sight of so much courage, cheerfulness, and devotion" left him too elated "to mind the infinite pity and horror of the sights."

I left Kalaupapa on the ten-minute flight to Kaunakakai. The route gave me a last look at the contours of the north shore. I had come to this moody, windswept land of misty sea cliffs and verdant valleys to experience its rugged beauty. But more than anything I would remember the people who shared with me a little of the rich heritage of the Hawaiians. Their voices, like the sigh of the unceasing wind and the rumble of surf, bring vitality and poetry to the north shore.

Following Pages: Old ways pass to the young. Elder Kupuna Lani Kapuni shows great-grandniece Mellisa how to gather limu, *or seaweed, a traditional task and fare for Hawaiian women, for whom many other foods were taboo.*

TALK

Refuge or prison? Kalaupapa Peninsula on Molokai's north shore became both in the 19th century for victims of leprosy. A lantana blossom on a beach and the Siloama

Catholic Church hint at a tranquillity that belies the pain that once permeated this place. In the early days, unfortunates who contracted the scourge dwelt here in appalling conditions. Now a few elderly residents, their disease arrested by modern medicines, remain by their own choice. And Kalaupapa National Historical Park commemorates a bittersweet chapter in Hawaii's story.

A worker in Waipi'o Valley on the Big Island pulls weeds in a taro patch. Another cultivator (opposite) holds up harvested plants, called kalo *in Hawaiian. From the rootlike corms, cooked and pounded into paste, comes poi, once the mainstay of the Hawaiian diet. In ancient times, a sacred calendar governed cultivation, deeming a full moon propitious for weeding the crop. Interest in growing taro increases as Hawaiians look to their heritage.*

FOLLOWING PAGES: *Cliffs in the remote North Kohala region of the Big Island march to the sea, as horses and mules graze in the fading rays of evening.*

Not Far from the City

Mist and drizzle had given way to broken white clouds, but the wind still shook rain from the trees. Sunlight and shadow accented the ridges and ravines that rippled the slopes of the Waianae Range into folds like billows of drapery. To the east, across the Schofield Plateau, the Koolau Range rose abruptly, its pinnacles and weathered curves devoured by distance and fused into a single, broad silhouette.

I was in the Waianaes on the way to the summit of 4,025-foot Mount Kaala, Oahu's highest peak. The trail starts in woodlands about an hour's drive from the throngs and skyscrapers of Honolulu and ends in a cloud forest of diminutive trees. The daylong hike took me a world away from 7-Elevens and Tiffanys and gave me a small window on the landscapes of Hawaii's distant past—a time before beach blankets or even human footprints intruded on the sands of Waikiki.

It's incredible that Oahu still harbors pockets of wilderness. The island has less than 10 percent of the land area of the state but about four-fifths of its 1.1 million residents. On the average, an additional 80,000 visitors crowd the island every day. The urban areas extend beyond Honolulu, a city of 836,000, and a steady stream of traffic fills the freeways that connect the capital with Kailua, Kaneohe, and Pearl City. Much of the remaining land is devoted to sugarcane and pineapple plantations and to the Department of Defense, which occupies a fourth of the island.

In earlier times, valleys were turned into taro paddies. With the arrival of haoles, forests were logged for sandalwood and stripped for firewood to process whale blubber. Grazing cattle denuded other tracts. As the forest cover shrank, the watershed declined, and streams and springs began drying up. Rains were washing the bare mountain slopes away. To deal with the crisis, large-scale reforestation projects were launched as early as the 1890s. Foresters planted whatever would grow quickly, blitzing the islands with the seeds and seedlings of nearly a thousand introduced plants.

Those who mourn the lost landscapes of Hawaii criticize these foresters for their "Johnny Appleseed mentality" and their notion that it's best to plant something—just anything. Others point out that the early foresters were trying to save areas that were eroding—and succeeded. Protecting native Hawaiian ecosystems was not a priority until the 1970s.

Somehow, fragments of distinctly Hawaiian forests and seashores survive, much as nature built them—even on beleaguered Oahu. To protect some of these unspoiled, unique landscapes on state lands, Hawaii established the Natural Area Reserves System (NARS) in 1970. It is managed by Hawaii's Department of Land and Natural Resources and now counts 19

reserves on five islands. One of these sits on the summit of Mount Kaala, the first of my destinations in Oahu's backcountry.

I had not progressed far up the trail when I heard dogs barking in the distance. "They're after a wild pig," explained Steven Montgomery, the conservation biologist who was leading the hike for the Bishop Museum. "The hunters are in there, too, crashing through the brush and following the sound. The barking becomes sharper and more urgent when the dogs have cornered the pig. Then hunters release their other dogs to help hold the pig until the men catch up."

As the sounds of the chase faded away, Steve described the final stages of the hunt, when the maddened, squealing pig lunges at the dogs, trying to slash them with its tusks. "Sometimes the dogs are gored in the struggle, and most hunters carry needle and thread to sew them up."

A versatile scientist in his mid-40s, Steve has a mild manner and a studious look, but on Hawaii's steep slopes he has the agility and endurance of a professional athlete. He hunts pigs as well as goats, for food and also because they are so destructive of native landscapes.

But Steve is far more intent on other pursuits. He analyzes the gizzards of birds to learn what bugs they eat. He prowls the forests at night, when stealthy, nocturnal insects move about. He lies prone on the ground to examine plants leaf by leaf, searching for creatures so minute, so cryptic, or so well camouflaged that few scientists previously knew they existed. Thus far, Steve has found about 80 species new to science, including 10 kinds of ambushing inchworms, known as killer caterpillars. New insects show up all the time. Steve estimates that only two-thirds of Hawaii's fauna have been identified, so the end of discoveries is nowhere in sight.

An entomologist by training, Steve also has a good eye for plants, and botanists have named one of his finds in the daisy family *Remya montgomeryi,* a species with no more than a hundred individual plants left.

These days Steve gives top priority to Hawaii's extinction crisis, devoting his energy to saving what is left of native environments. So that others may know and care, he also leads his public outings into the mountains for the Bishop Museum and the Conservation Council for Hawaii, sharing his enthusiasm with those who scramble after him on the slopes.

FOLLOWING PAGES: Powerful breaking waves curl onto Oahu's sparsely developed north shore in winter. Although a mecca for surfers, the tranquil region provides a marked contrast to bustling Honolulu.

GARY HOFHEIMER / DOUGLAS PEEBLES PHOTOGRAPHY

The lower reaches of the trail were littered with Brazilian strawberry guava. I found the sweet, apple-crisp fruit very tasty, and my fingers were soon stained purple from gluttony. Unfortunately, pigs like them, too, and their droppings sow the guava seeds throughout the forest.

"To make matters worse the strawberry guava is extremely aggressive," said Steve. "Apparently it competes by using chemical warfare. When the leaves rot, they exude a substance that inhibits the germination of other seeds. You can see what happens," he added, pointing to rank upon rank of slender saplings that left no room for other plants.

"At home in Brazil the tree has natural enemies, but here there are no controls to keep it in check. What we need is some very picky Brazilian insect that eats nothing but strawberry guava. We'd have to make sure by lab testing that it would rather starve than switch to eating anything else."

As we moved higher up the mountain, a mix of shrubs and trees broke the monoculture of strawberry guava. Ti plants were scattered across the hillside, each like a fly whisk with an elegant plume of long, shiny, green leaves. A member of the agave family, the ti plant provided ancient Hawaiians with an edible root, raincoats, plates, foil for baking fish, and medicines. It also served as an amulet. Even now it is used as a wrapper for cooking food. I liked it best as a cool compress against my sweaty brow.

Even more valuable was the kukui, esteemed in old Hawaiian chants and now honored as Hawaii's state tree. Its branches sprawl and twist like those of a venerable oak; its fruit looks like a chestnut and burns like a candle. Ancient Hawaiians skewered the nuts on the spines of coconut fronds, making shish kebabs of them to light their homes. I wondered if Hawaiian parents set bedtimes at two or three kukui nuts after dark.

Both the ti and kukui came to Hawaii aboard the double canoes carrying settlers from the Marquesa and Society Islands, almost 2,500 miles away. The boats were Polynesian biospheres, outfitted with pigs, dogs, chickens, and crop plants to stock the new land. The cargo included sweet potatoes, yams, breadfruit, bananas, sugarcane, and taro. Even the coconut palm arrived on board, in the form of nuts.

Steve halted before a small native tree called *pāpala kēpau.* Rather nondescript, I thought, until I learned that its seeds are as sticky as flypaper. For the tree, the gum is a dispersal strategy; for the ancient Hawaiians, it was glue they smeared on branches to catch birds for their plumage.

High-ranking nobility wore feather cloaks and helmets and possessed feathered idols that were marvels of painstaking work. Tiny feathers, tied to a fine-meshed net, formed a surface as lustrous as velvet. Wrapped in an ʻiʻiwi cape, one 19th-century visiting chief dazzled Bostonians as he "moved up State Street like a living flame," according to an eyewitness.

With as many as 450,000 feathers used to make one large cloak, countless forest birds landed in harm's way. Some islanders believe that a few feathers were plucked from a bird, and then it was released. Hawaiian scholars hold that many of the birds were plucked, cooked, and eaten.

Overhunting probably played a small role in the decline of species like the now extinct *mamo* and ʻōʻō, which were prized for their feathers.

"In fact," said Steve, "at least 35 bird species became extinct in the 1,500 years before the Europeans arrived."

This news, which stunned Hawaiian paleontologists, comes from a series of fossil discoveries over the last 16 years. Steve summarized the findings. Bones unearthed from kitchen middens revealed that some of these vanished species—large flightless geese and ducks—were killed for food. Other discoveries point the finger at Hawaiian agriculture, which destroyed the lowland forest habitat, and also at the frequent burning of wild lowlands to promote the growth of *pili* grass for thatch.

While Steve meandered across the themes of Hawaiian history and biology as nimbly as he moved up the mountain, he was also showing me things it took his practiced eye to see: a communal web produced by several spiders pooling their silk; a klepto-parasitic spider that pilfers from the webs of others; a whirligig mite that moves so quickly that Steve calls it the cheetah of mite society; and terrestrial, shrimplike crustaceans that moved upstream to higher elevations and now breathe air.

Conversation was curtailed after lunch, when the climb began in earnest, and the trail became a track following a narrow ridge. I edged past sheer drops and labored up inclines still slick with mud from a recent rain. Fixed ropes had been installed on the steepest pitches for hikers, but it was slow going as I hung on and pulled myself up.

Steve pointed to a trio of iridescent dragonflies.

"They are the hawks of the insect world, patrolling the ridgeline for something to eat. They're looking for bugs lifted up here by air currents."

I nodded as I caught my breath.

"At least in Hawaii you don't have to worry about snakes and leeches when you reach up for a handhold," Steve said cheerfully.

I did, however, need gloves as a protection against Florida blackberry. Its nasty, prickly branches were another hazard of the trail, and they left bleeding scratch marks wherever my bare arms brushed against them.

"It makes me feel good just to whack or pull at the noxious things," said Steve, yanking at a small clump while waiting for me to catch up. "I can't help wondering what Hawaiian plant it has displaced."

The last rise put us on the tableland of the summit, and we entered the Mount Kaala Natural Area Reserve, a ferny, green profusion rooted in the scant soil that lay beneath the ooze of the bog. We looked out across a solid mass of vegetation growing low to the ground, with a scattering of small ohia and *lapalapa* trees. The ohias were miniature, and their branches, mottled with thick lichens and feathery liverworts, reached little more than head high. "If the trees were taller, winds would blow them over, because roots can't anchor well in thin soil like this," said Steve.

Though scarlet tufts blossomed among the ohia's dark green leaves, the branches, gnarled as a witch's fingers, gave the trees a melancholy look. Perhaps it was the contrast with the lapalapa trees, whose leaves fluttered gaily at every breeze. The signature plant of the high-altitude bog forest, the lapalapas were as slender as bamboo stalks, with pale, quivering leaves.

We crossed the bog on a boardwalk bordered by ferns, pūkiawe, and

Limpid waters and soft breezes off Lanikai Beach offer serene pleasures on

saxifrage laden in the summer season with showy pink flowers that flared above large, fuzzy leaves. Blackberry, which had plagued us on the upper trail, was nowhere in sight. Until recently, the reserve's 60-acre summit bog also had been infested with it, but a NARS eradication program, helped by volunteers, knocked the thickets back; workers hacked the plants off at the base and dripped herbicide on the cuts. It's one of the latest success stories in the combat against weeds in Hawaii.

"It was a small, well-defined area of vigorous native ecosystem. With a little help and a lot of work from volunteers, the Hawaiian plants could regenerate," explained Steve.

A corner of the summit is claimed by FAA and military radar stations, which put a high-tech mushroom field of receivers alongside the pocket-size wilderness. Somehow the intrusion didn't bother me much. The abiding images of the day are of things I had never seen before: the blithe dance

windward Oahu. Highways link this area to Honolulu, state capital and tourist hub.

of lapalapa leaves; a white serpentine line on a leaf that was a tunnel made by a caterpillar mining chlorophyll; a cricket hiding in a hollow twig; and a tree snail with a spiraled, banded shell less than an inch in diameter.

It is one of the many species of tree snails on the brink of extinction. In the 19th century they were so numerous that a European naturalist visiting Oahu observed, "nature has placed countless land snails instead of insects on the leaves of trees." Another naturalist noted that shell collecting became a popular "sport," and snails were picked "from trees and low bushes as rapidly as one would gather huckleberries from a prolific field." One scientist accumulated an estimated 44,500 shells in two years. Other hoards also numbered in the tens of thousands.

Some collections were donated to the University of Hawaii, and I had an opportunity to look at those stored in one of the laboratories where Professor of Zoology Michael G. Hadfield *(Continued on page 159)*

In a lush, ferny world above Honolulu's sprawl, hikers explore the Mānoa Valley in the Koolau Range. Although Oahu has more than 80 percent of the state's population, wilderness endures on the slopes of mountains too steep for agriculture, logging, or grazing cattle. Now fast-spreading alien plants threaten to crowd out endemic species. Prized for their shells, Achatinellidae tree snails (left) were collected by the thousand in the 19th century. But introduced predators are by far the greatest threat to these endangered species.

Imports from South America, Jatropha *blossoms and feathery* Myriophyllum *add beauty*

to a woodland pond. The water feather has spread from gardens as an aquatic weed.

Sunrise burnishes ridges of the Koolau Range honed sharp by rain. Trade winds bring moisture-laden air to windward slopes. In Hawaii's benign tropical climate, many newcomer plants spread like wildfire. Sierra Club volunteers (above) work with a state biologist on Mount Kaala to control Florida blackberry. They will snip off shrubs, then apply a drop of herbicide to the base.

does his research. There were shells of dozens of species of the Achatinellidae family of snails, banded in various soft colors. The empty coils in my hands had once been inhabited by a variety of snails, all living in the same way. Each one probably spent its whole life in a single tree, feeding on the film of mold that forms on leaves. The species differ only in the shape and patterns of the shell.

"There's nothing adaptive about changes on the shell," said Michael. "There's no survival value in a yellow band over one that is green. Yet the diversity of these Hawaiian land snails represents one of the most extraordinary examples of speciation in the world. We can only wonder why so many forms evolved, when all are doing the same thing."

Today, of the original thousand species, there are fewer than 200 left.

"The worst threat to the surviving populations comes from a carnivorous snail from Florida, *Euglandina rosea,* introduced in 1955," said Michael. "A cannibal snail, it was imported to control the African snail, which arrived in the 1930s and had become a major garden pest. Unfortunately, *Euglandina* is more interested in the harmless native snails, which it devours by forcing its muscular proboscis into the shell opening and swallowing the animal inside. I'm not entirely sure what role tree snails play in the forest ecology. But a thousand species of terrestrial snails must have represented a significant factor. If you lose all thousand species, you forfeit a lot of life's diversity."

The man in charge of preserving and improving what's left of Oahu's natural legacy on state lands is biologist David G. Smith, manager of the island's reserves. A haole in his 30s who remembers when Honolulu had few buildings taller than its poinciana trees, Dave is in the front line of the struggle to halt the march of weeds. He's also trying to restore native ecosystems, something that hasn't been attempted until very recently. Like all land managers, he's writing the book as he goes along.

"You have to write off some areas so saturated with seeds of introduced plants that there's no hope of eradicating them," said Dave, as we started up the Poamoho Ridge Trail in the Koolau Range.

The 3.4-mile path through some of the wildest rain forest on Oahu ascends the Koolau and is one of the spur trails that intersects with what will become the 20-mile Koolau Summit Trail. Together with feeder trails, it eventually will form a major route in Hawaii's statewide system called Na Ala Hele—Trails for Walking. Under the program, established in 1988, the state will secure access rights across private lands and improve and stitch together many of the existing trails into a broad network.

With rainfall averaging well over a hundred inches a year and

Retrieved as an egg from an abandoned nest, an endangered Hawaiian black-necked stilt strolls in the Honolulu Zoo. The facility also holds animals confiscated by state inspectors who check for illegal imports.

greenhouse temperatures, trails in the Koolaus grow over quickly. Keeping them open is a job as endless as the labors of Sisyphus. A crew was scheduled to swing machetes along the Poamoho Trail, and Dave was flagging plants that should not be cut.

"We'll detour around an ohia or make hikers duck under its branches, but if it's *Clidemia,* we'll cut it back five feet from the trail," said Dave.

Among the most reviled of the invaders, *Clidemia* is a Central American shrub that has spread like wildfire through Oahu. It obliterates the natural understory, reducing it to a mass of crimped, yellow-green leaves.

"A large plant releases a million minute seeds. In some areas you can find an overgrown trail simply by tracking *Clidemia,* which has come in in the mud of hikers' boots," said Dave.

No one sees a way of eradicating this prolific weed once it's established, but a new weapon, biological control, may keep it in check. A fungus from Panama and insects from Trinidad damage the plant and nothing else. They are beginning to have some effect, said Dave, but biocontrol is a long-term thing.

There was some *Clidemia* along the Poamoho Trail, but it had not displaced the dense cover of uluhe ferns that wrapped the landscape in an unbroken blanket of emerald green. "We're seeing so much uluhe because the area is so steep. It moves into places where there's a lot of slumping," Dave explained. Hawaiians called uluhe "the healer" because it quickly covers bare ground. Hikers who have to thrash or hack through it call it something else.

The trail was rather easy going, but around us the terrain was cut to pieces by deep gulches. Ridges were honed to narrow crests and carved with so many spires, grooves, and scallops that the Koolaus seemed as malleable as sculptor's clay. With steep pitches and dense vegetation, the panorama was one best seen by a butterfly.

In the verdant ravines, the only bright color came from the ohia flowers. Other blossoms were more discreet—like the slender *'ākia* with tiny yellow trumpets hanging beneath the leaves. Many of Hawaii's trees evolved flowers to capture the attention of stealthy insect pollinators and not birds, or mammals, or spectators like me.

Dave kept an eye out for invading weeds, to take them out before they had a chance to get established.

"Even if I can't identify the plant, I can tell it's an exotic, because it just doesn't seem to fit into the landscape. A native forest is a mosaic of species growing together in a balanced state. Everything seems to have a sense of place. Take the vines. Native ones just use the trees to climb up to the light, whereas the smothering banana *poka* is not so well-behaved. It's so aggressive it doesn't know when to stop."

Trade winds had been blowing hard all morning, herding wispy clouds across the sky like flocks of migrant birds. When we reached the summit ridge, the wind was gusting at 60 miles an hour. Though we were only at 2,500 feet, a regime of heavy winds had scraped the mountain spine to a tundra emptiness. Short grasses and sedges shivered, and the ubiquitous ohias, with their stunted and scraggly branches, seemed to cower before the pummeling blasts.

Afternoon often brings a heavy bank of clouds that lands on the summit ridge and snuffs out the view. But on that August day, facing up to a whiplash of winds, we could look down on miles of sinuous windward coast scalloped by bays and coves. Sharp descents looked sleek and smooth under a mantle of uluhe that buried jackstraws of fallen trees and slope irregularities. From this distance, the surf was a cursive white line between the aqua shallows and an expanse of ocean as dark as ink.

The sweeping view was ours alone until two hikers rounded the knoll to the summit. They were the only people we encountered along the way.

Another escape from crowds lies upon a sun-scorched finger of black lava and pale sand called Kaena Point. This westernmost piece of Oahu confronts the island's wildest waters. At its tip, a 32-acre site—Kaena Point—was classified a natural area reserve in 1983. By Hawaiian tradition, it is the place where the souls of Oahu's dead begin their journey to the land of their ancestors. By modern practice, Kaena Point became a graveyard for skeletal cars stripped of everything but rust. It was also a recreation area for the hot-rodders with jeeps, motorbikes, and dune buggies who were crushing the low-growing coastal plants and demolishing the dunes.

As I walked the two and a half miles from the highway to the reserve, I grieved at the damage that wheels and litter had done. Even the sight of combers curling out of the indigo sea in great green arcs and striking the rocks in bursts of foam did not distract me from the disagreeable scene.

But once I crossed into the reserve, the landscape changed. Volunteers have cleared the trash away, and Dave Smith has kept vehicles out by building a 75-foot-long rock wall.

Now Kaena Point is a prime example of native plants on the rebound. Beach naupaka grows like crabgrass, holding dunes in its green grasp. Other coastal plants are also coming back, and, with their delicately beautiful flowers spangling the ground, they are a lure for walking. Their leaves are a lesson in ways to fend off the harsh sunlight and desiccating winds. Some are succulent and store water; some have waxy surfaces that reduce evaporation; others have surfaces that reflect the light.

Another sign of Kaena Point's recovery is the return of the Laysan albatross. A set of birds had nested there in the spring. I hoped to see them as I strolled past the low dunes to the lighthouse at the peninsula tip. But it was summer, and the albatross chick had obviously tried its wings successfully, and the family had flown away. The strong wind carried only the silence of the sand and stone and the muted rumble of the breaking sea.

There are shorter jaunts in the forests just outside Honolulu city limits that are also a refuge from crowds and concrete. Every mile on the trails in the Makiki Valley and Mount Tantalus area is a short course in world botany and bird life. Descendants of African plants that began Hawaii's coffee industry survive in forests of dizzying diversity. Native koa and ohia trees grow alongside Southeast Asian kukui, bamboo, and mountain apple, as well as Chinese banyans, Australian eucalyptus, African tulip trees, and Norfolk Island pines. From one perspective, they are arboreal examples of the East rubbing shoulders with the West, mirroring in a way Hawaii's extraordinary mosaic of cultures.

Shama thrushes sing the flutelike melodies they brought from Malaysia. Mynahs from India, mockingbirds from North America, Brazilian cardinals, Japanese white-eyes, and Java sparrows give the forests voices as varied as the languages in the streets of Honolulu. The diversity is enchanting, but this assortment of birds and medley of songs have come at a price. Competition for space and food and the spread of avian malaria and pox have cost many Hawaiian birds their lives.

One February day I found a little solitude on the Mānoa Cliffs Trail. The coffee trees looked like fallen clouds, with their masses of white

"We drain the pool to catch the Hawaiian monk seal pups and grab the end that doesn't bite," says curator Marlee Breese at Sea Life Park on Oahu.

flowers. The yellow guavas were in fruit, flavoring the air with perfume. I returned again in August, when the dazzle belonged to the white native hibiscus, each tree an explosion of large, lavish white blossoms. Their great beauty had not yet been overrun and displaced.

For the time being, these imperiled survivors are holding their ground. However, as in the plea of Dr. Seuss's Lorax, it seems "perfectly clear" that "UNLESS someone…cares a whole awful lot, nothing is going to get better. It's not." Throughout the islands there are many like Dave Smith and Steve Montgomery who are striving to save Hawaii's special legacy of plants and animals. It seems perfectly clear that unless they succeed, an essential part of America's tropical paradise will be lost forever.

Handlers must force-feed such orphans because they haven't learned to catch fish. After a year they will be released in the Northwestern Hawaiian Islands.

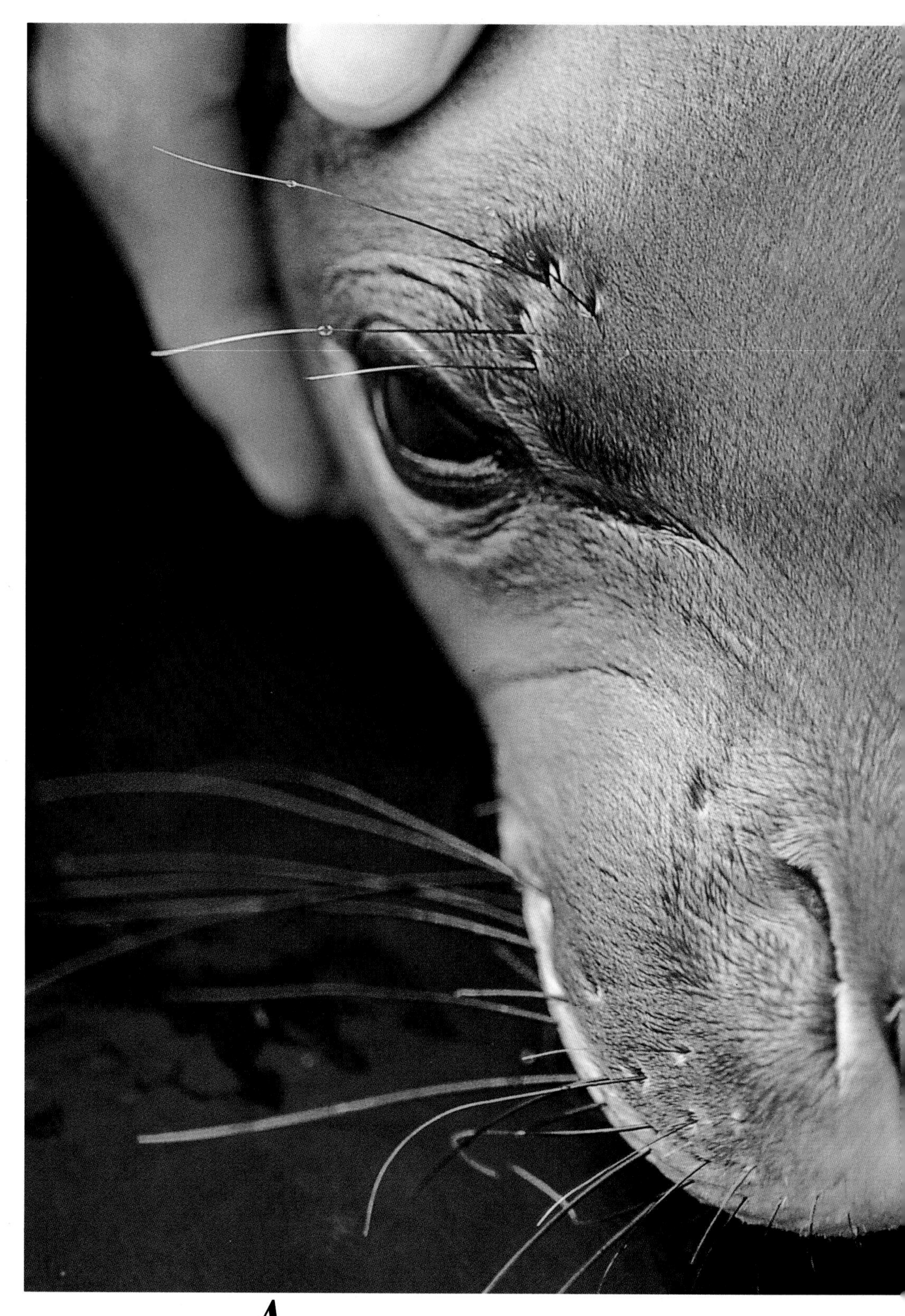

An endangered species laid low by humans, a monk seal orphan pup now depends upon human hands for survival.

FOLLOWING PAGES: Walls of an eroded crater embrace Oahu's Hanauma Bay. Its coral reefs, protected by strict regulations, draw legions of snorkelers and divers.

Safeguarding bird life at Kaena Point Natural Area Reserve on Oahu, biologist David Smith removes a mongoose trapped at the site. The weasel-like animal, imported from India in 1883 to prey on rats, feeds largely on eggs and chicks instead. Trails scar dune vegetation (right) at Kaena Point. Banning vehicles has allowed plants to begin making a comeback.

FOLLOWING PAGES: *In the waters of Hanauma Bay, coral provides a homeland for sea life. Erosion's murky silt now threatens some offshore corals.*

In the Shadow of Mount

On Kauai, where one of the wettest spots on earth lies within 20 miles of parched scrub, landscapes are so wonderfully diverse that it is hard to believe the small island contains them all. Runoff from the torrential rainfall on Mount Waialeale pours straight down the mountain's steep face, falling in cascades that gleam like columns of crystal in the wind-spun mist. In contrast, water runs dark and sluggish in the Alaka'i Swamp on the summit's gentle face, where mosses as sodden as sponges swathe stunted trees.

Tropical jungles flourish in balmy valleys not far from groves of stately redwoods and pines that call to mind the conifer forests of the American West. Fields of sugarcane rippling in the wind dominate the fertile coastal plains, which also yield coffee and taro. Another sort of crop is harvested from the arid, sun-baked flats in the southwest, where Hawaiians have evaporated and collected sea salt for centuries.

Little grows on the sculptured ramparts of Waimea Canyon, which Mark Twain called "the Grand Canyon of the Pacific." Vegetation puts only a green scribble on its sheer walls, and in the ever changing light the iron-reds and ochers of the rock become a kaleidoscope of color.

Kauai offers Hawaii in microcosm, with an amazing range of climates and terrain that became a separate stage for the evolution of plants and animals. The island also summed up for me the loveliness of Hawaii's landscapes and the vulnerability of its natural environment. For like the other islands, Kauai is haunted by an ecological crisis threatening to wipe out its native flora and fauna.

One of the last strongholds for native forest birds is the Alaka'i Wilderness Preserve on a high plateau on the lee of Waialeale's 5,148-foot crest. It has remained relatively pristine because of the ruggedness of its terrain. At the summit, annual rainfall averages nearly 500 inches—more than 40 feet! "The supersaturated land at the very top is as barren as arctic tundra," said wildlife biologist Tom Telfer. "In that wet gloom a few specialized plants grow among the clumps of pale sedges."

A member of Kauai's Division of Forestry and Wildlife, Tom was checking conditions along the Alaka'i Trail, which cuts across the lower reaches of the reserve. There rain tapers off to about 240 inches a year, still considerably more than New York City's 44-inch annual average.

"Traditionally, the Alaka'i has been labeled a swamp, but it's something of a misnomer," explained Tom, as we drove up the mountain on Highway 550 to the trailhead on the eastern boundary of Kōke'e State Park.

"The Alaka'i doesn't have the stretches of open, standing water that characterize a swamp. Instead, there's a mix of rain forest and occasional

pockets of bog, formed where water doesn't drain through the impermeable clay and rock. Actual bog areas constitute less than 2 percent of the swamp."

We had started on the sunny coast with a partial view of Waialeale and its almost permanent cap of clouds. But within 20 miles, as we set out on the five-mile Alaka'i Trail, we were engulfed in a chill gray drizzle as fine as mist.

A narrow boardwalk made our first two miles an easy walk. The gray clouds lay so low they blotted out most of the landscape. The trees on the higher, drier ground were shadows, many with the ohia's unmistakable silhouette of long, twisting branches.

The stunted vegetation in the bogs is a muted tapestry, mostly sedges, grasses, ferns, and dwarf ohias, called in Hawaiian "ohias of the mist." The versatile ohias do not seem to require much to prosper, and in that vaporous world their scarlet-tufted blossoms, called ohia lehua, seemed more voluptuous than ever. Though some ohias were only inches tall, the flowers were the same full-blown sprays that bring beauty to a hundred-foot tree.

Heathery pūkiawe and 'ōhelo were also part of the matted turf. Lily-like *Astelia* formed small clusters of silver-green strap leaves. Violets grew as vines, trailing heart-shaped foliage across the ground. Other vines belonged to a plant in the coffee family, called *kūkae-nēnē* because its black fruit look like nene droppings. The insect-eating sundews were so small I didn't notice them until Tom pointed to the miniature leaves beaded with sticky red resin. These elaborate bits of flypaper really need a hand lens to be appreciated. The leaves not only snare insects but also release enzymes that dissolve them, so the plant can consume its prey.

We entered a section of forest upholstered in mosses. They wrapped the ohias and lay in cushions on the ground. When I grasped a branch, it dribbled water. The bough seemed the diameter of my arm, but inside the casing of moss it was the size of a twig.

After two miles, just as we started across a bog, the trail ran out of boardwalk. Puddles multiplied and plant species declined, reducing the mosaic to patches of ferns, stunted ohias, and the dark sheen of still water.

It was slow going, sinking knee-deep in mud. I tried to seek spots where ohias were taller, for they were clues to higher ground. A few inches of elevation were enough to give the ohias more height and to lift me out

FOLLOWING PAGES: Receding storm unveils Kauai's Kalalau Valley. Such mountains are home to Hawaii's menehune, mythical "little people" that islanders credit with public works: ditching, damming, and building roads.

FRANS LANTING / MINDEN PICTURES

of the deeper ooze. But as Tom predicted, I soon didn't care how muddy I got, and I just squished through the muck.

"We're going to build the boardwalk to the end of the trail," said Tom. "Partly to keep people from straying off the path. It's easy to get lost here because of dense fog and the lack of distinct landmarks. There's also real danger of falling into drop-offs that are hidden by the tangled vegetation. A few years ago two experienced hikers disappeared. We searched and searched but never found a trace.

"The boardwalk also keeps people from trampling the thin, fragile plant cover. You use a trail a few times and it turns into a pigsty. Even a few footsteps can leave long-lasting scars and open sites for weeds to sprout. Basically, we're trying to manage the area for low human impact to protect the endangered forest birds. For them the Alaka'i is a last refuge."

The future of the Hawaiian honeycreepers and others may depend on the scientists who are trying to learn more about the life cycle and behavior of these forest songbirds.

"We know so very little about their biology. For starters, we need to get some idea of when and at what age they breed, what percentage of the young die, how long chicks stay with parents, and how long adults live," said Dr. Stuart Pimm, professor of ecology at the University of Tennessee.

"To understand why a species is dying out, you need to know whether the casualties are the young birds or adults. Current research is urgently trying to find out what the birds need and what they're not getting."

Tom and I came upon Stuart and his assistants in the Alaka'i, where they were mist-netting and color-banding birds so they could monitor individuals through binoculars. They had just caught a small yellow-green '*amakihi* in a gossamer net stretched between two trees. One of the researchers was lowering the almost invisible net like a flag on a flagpole.

"These 'amakihi, like the other honeycreepers, appear surprisingly long-lived. For example, on the mainland a small bird like this has a life expectancy of only a year. Researchers on the Big Island have tracked banded honeycreepers from one year to the next. Some of the honeycreepers are still feeding their young when the chicks are nearly two years old. So the adults have to live much longer than that," Stuart told us, as he disentangled the bird from the fine mesh.

Before touching the bird, he had washed his hands with disinfectant, and as he held the 'amakihi, he fed it some sugar water through an eyedropper. It seemed remarkably calm. Before banding and releasing the bird, Stuart also took a blood sample to check for malaria parasites.

Native forest birds have little resistance to avian malaria, which is common among continental birds. But, says Stuart, the impact of avian malaria in Hawaii is difficult to pin down. Some scientists believe the disease is the number one culprit making Hawaii's rate of bird extinctions the world's highest. They assert it's no coincidence that very few native species survive at lower elevations, where the malaria-carrying mosquito breeds.

"It's hard getting a good handle on all the reasons behind the bird extinctions and die-offs," says Tom. "There are probably some causes we don't even know about yet. Every level of the environment is threatened, and sometimes the problem is oversimplified. Some people would like to think that if they only eradicate goats and pigs, things will return to normal. But if you get rid of them, aggressive weeds move in. Some are so invasive and numerous that there is no hope of eradicating them. Millions of seeds on the ground are a biological time bomb ready to explode."

Tom believes it might be better to limit the number of goats through public hunting and by fencing isolated rare plants for propagation.

Botanist Steven Perlman disagrees.

"Sure, goats might keep some of the weeds down, but if you don't remove them, there aren't going to be many rare plants left. It's devastating to come upon animals chewing on the last few survivors of a species," said Steve, a scientist who locates, monitors, and collects seeds to propagate the 372 plants on Hawaii's rare and endangered list.

Steve works for the Hawaii Plant Conservation Center at Kauai's National Tropical Botanical Garden, one of the few tropical plant research facilities in the country. With his partner, Ken Wood, he specializes in cliff habitats. He explores places too steep even for goats by rappelling down sheer faces and finding a way down precipitous ridges so thick with vegetation it seems impossible to get through. This high-risk research has brought unexpected results. So far the team has discovered 17 species never seen before and found 16 plants that had been listed as extinct.

"Cliffs are definitely the last frontier for Hawaiian botany," said Steve, looping a rope around a tree. He was about to lower himself down a sharp incline to check an obscure member of the daisy family found nowhere but on this dry ridge on the road to Kōke'e State Park.

In this case, Steve's mission was to collect seeds. The center gives top priority to propagating rare and endangered plants. "There's an urgent need to cultivate a lot of these plants. They're dying right now or will be extinct within five or ten years if we do nothing. They are not going to make it on their own," said Steve, after hauling himself back up the ridge.

"We don't want to just put these species in botanical gardens. That's a short-term remedy—a temporary Band-Aid, so we don't lose them. The goal is to return them to their natural home, but the problem of weeds and browsing animals can't be solved quickly, so we need to put small enclosure fences around these rare plants."

For the next few hours I followed Steve as he made his rounds. He cut smothering blackberry vines away from one plant to give it a place in the sun. He worried about the well-being of another. Several of his wards had produced flowers but had not set seeds, probably because they had lost their pollinators. In these cases, the plants got a little help from Steve, who used a fine brush to transfer pollen from one flower to another, granting life to a new generation.

Kōke'e's main road leads to the Kalalau Lookout, with its vista of the great amphitheater valley plunging 3,000 feet to the Pacific. Tier after tier of skeletal ridges arch out from the flanking walls like flying buttresses and fall abruptly to Kalalau's forested floor.

The traditional route into the valley is the Kalalau Trail in the Na Pali Coast State Park. The trail is generally considered the ultimate hiking trip in Hawaii. For 11 miles it meanders along a roadless stretch of coast. It climbs up and down hills, dawdles in lush valleys, teeters on cliffs high above the sea, and traverses slickrock slopes.

To understand the magic of the trail takes only a look at the panoramic views along the way. As far as the eye can see, a tranquil procession of huge, sculptured cliffs curves down to the rippled blue of the Pacific. At times I was immobilized by the sheer drama of the landscape, a work of art on a staggering scale. The soaring, fluted escarpments, pinnacles, and spires seemed like a masterpiece of medieval architecture. For Manfred Grabner, a visitor from Graz, Austria, the scenery conjured the sounds of a symphony underscored by the drumbeats of the sea.

"It is not Mozart, not Bartók. I hear Beethoven," he told me.

Manfred carried a camera, but he was not taking pictures.

"The impression is too big. I would like to show my friends this beauty, but the screen for my slides is too small to encompass this scene."

At Ke'e Beach, where the Kalalau Trail begins, I could see 1,500-foot Makana Cliff. In centuries past, Hawaiians celebrated great events by hurling firebrands of dried pāpala or *hau* branches from those heights. Because the slope is concave, trade winds are funneled upward. Smoldering sticks caught in these updrafts were fanned into a blaze and burned in the darkness until finally they fell to sea like meteors.

I heard about these Hawaiian fireworks from David Boynton, an enthusiastic naturalist and a science teacher who heads Kauai's environmental education program. Dave has campaigned against resort developments that would bulldoze some of Hawaii's last remaining wild coastlines into manicured golf courses, concrete waterfalls, and swimming-pool bars.

A knowledgeable companion with an easy, folksy manner, Dave told me about the lacewing larva that looks like a bit of lichen because it wears the exoskeleton of its insect prey. We saw *'o'opu,* fish that inhabit the upper reaches of streams and reverse the migration behavior of salmon: They swim *down* to estuaries to spawn. The fry migrate back up, using fused fins on their bellies like suction cups to latch onto the mossy walls of waterfalls.

Dave spotted a cluster of *Brighamia insignis* anchored in crevices of the cliff. A severely endangered species, the bizarre-looking plant resembles a cabbage on a squat, fleshy stem.

Many of the large ti plants and banana and kukui trees were the very ones planted by early Hawaiians who had lived in the valleys of the Na Pali coast. They were reminders that Hawaiian farmers and fishermen had walked this trail for a thousand years.

In Hanakāpi'ai Valley, the first of five valleys intersecting the trail, we stumbled across stone walls, the remains of ancient taro terraces. "Every available inch of land was cultivated. The Hawaiians were masters of irrigation and of converting wilderness to agriculture," said Dave, as we followed the spur trail into the narrow, verdant valley.

Terrace walls made the areas of taro cultivation easy to identify. An acre of wet taro will support 15 people. Archaeologists use this ratio to calculate the population of the islands before the fatal contact with Europeans. On this basis, pre-1778 population estimates for the islands range from 200,000 up to 600,000. Today, of more than 1.1 million residents, no more than 140,000 count themselves as at least 50 percent Hawaiian.

We saw an occasional taro plant as we ascended the narrowing valley, but mango and coffee trees were more in evidence. Wild ginger popped up in shady places, sporting a tall stalk with a waxy flowerhead like a reddish green pinecone, which fills with liquid scented by the flowers. In the muted light I could imagine tattooed women in tapa wraps picking the flowerheads to use the fragrant fluid as shampoo.

In Hanakāpi'ai's upper reaches, the whole valley boomed with the sound of water caroming down the headwall. On ledge after ledge for 300 feet, water exploded into foam and then fell again, creating a choreography of water in motion.

For the most strenuous segment of the hike, the next four miles to Hanakoa Valley, we had the company of Peter Kelly and his seven-year-old son, Collin. Pete spoke knowledgeably of the Kalalau's hippie era, when the valley attracted colorful characters.

The early contingent of newcomers in the valley included Jim Pfab, who came in the sixties, carrying only a Swiss army knife and a toothbrush. He lived off the land, gathering fruit, watercress, freshwater shrimp, and limpets. Today Jim is a computer engineer, and camping, he says, consists of sleeping with the bedroom window open.

The Robinson family, which owns the island of Niihau, grazed cattle in Kalalau until it became unprofitable. In 1970 the state acquired the valley and turned Kalalau into a park.

After more than an hour of uphill walking, we reached the highest point on the trail. It was no place for anyone with acrophobia. Inches from where we sat, like tropic birds on a perch, the ledge dropped straight down a dizzying 886 feet to the sea. Pete called the spot Space-out Rock.

Many gullies and slopes later, when the rich soil had turned to crumbly red slickrock and the vegetation had thinned out in the increasing aridity, we came to the crest of Red Hill. The whole glorious Kalalau Valley lay ahead. Beyond the cobble beach that gleamed darkly in the ebbing light, the broad stretch of white sand had turned to gold in the sunset. Shadows contoured the deeply eroded cliffs and ridges. Their elongated gothic shapes brought a cathedral aura to the valley.

Unfortunately that aura frequently is shattered by helicopters zipping sightseers along the coast. "Noise pollution has become a problem because competition is forcing tour operators to cut prices, which means they are cutting into flying time. With sufficient time you can avoid people and campsites," says Jack Harter, a pilot who started flight-seeing on Kauai in the early sixties.

In 1981 the state banned landings on the island's conservation lands. Places like the Na Pali coast are too fragile to have several companies shuttling visitors into the valleys all day long. *(Continued on page 186)*

With a deft brush, botanist Steve Perlman lends nature a hand, pollinating a unique plant called Brighamia insignis *in bloom on a sea cliff near Molokai's Hā'upu Bay. Some of Hawaii's more than 200 endangered endemic plants—like this* Brighamia*—survive only in such inaccessible sites, away from man and introduced plants and animals.* Brighamia*'s decline may have coincided with that of its natural pollinator, probably a moth. Clinging to the face of Huelo Islet (opposite), near Molokai, Perlman gathers* Brighamia *seeds for nursery propagation.*

WHIT BRONAUGH

Enchanted child of the forest in Hawaiian legend, the fruiting 'ie 'ie *brightens slopes of Mount Waialeale, the volcanic peak that formed Kauai (opposite). A stream (above) riffles through the Alaka'i Swamp, high on Waialeale. Nearly 500 inches of rainfall a year on the 5,148-foot peak—arguably the world's wettest place—help earn Kauai its nickname, the Garden Isle.*

FRANS LANTING / MINDEN PICTURES

Fern-filled verdure of the Alaka'i includes many of Hawaii's rarest plants

DAVID MUENCH

and birds. Such endemic species continue to intrigue biologists and botanists.

"But there's no better way to see how the very different landscapes of Kauai fit together, and helicopters take you where hikers can't go," says Jack. Many visitors agree.

Boating offers another view and another way to visit inaccessible places. The Na Pali coast extends nine miles beyond Kalalau to Polihale State Park, where the cliffs dwindle away to a beach, and the road begins.

Paddling a kayak seemed a more appropriate, Polynesian way to explore the quiet, isolated shore than skimming along in a motorboat. But as we pushed off into the wind chop and whitecaps I was not so sure.

"If the waves were really a problem, you wouldn't be able to see the horizon," said Chino Godinez, trying to reassure me. A world-class kayaker whose parents were refugees from Castro's Cuba, Chino and his brother Micco have made Kauai their home and kayaking a growing business.

"Riding the swells is no problem, unless you're prone to seasickness."

From time to time, green sea turtles paddled languidly alongside us, raising their heads occasionally to breathe. Then they would take off in a burst of speed, perhaps en route to French Frigate Shoals in the Northwestern Hawaiian Islands, where they breed and lay eggs.

High above, a great frigate bird soared in the wind, scarcely moving its long black wings. White-tailed tropic birds sailed along the cliffs like banners of surrender against the palette of green.

We camped on the sand at Kalalau, finding shelter in a shallow cave.

If hiking the trail and kayaking the coast are tests of endurance, a sojourn in the valley is an education in indolence. I began learning that afternoon. There was nothing I had to do. It was sufficient to watch the wind whip a thin veil of sand across the beach and to observe the big waves pound the shore and the surf bounce into fountains of spray.

Bathing in a waterfall just behind the beach is one of the pleasures of the valley. Another is a stroll at sunset, when the hoary bats flutter out to sea. Little is known about Hawaii's only native land mammal, but these small bats are regularly spotted 200 yards off the Na Pali coast. Biologists wonder what this small, insect-eating species is doing offshore.

By morning the ghost crabs had cleaned up the dinner crumbs we had left on the sand. Though a rampart of gray clouds to the northeast and a flat black sea warned of rain, we headed up the valley. The path snaked in and out of Kalalau Stream and around thickets of hau. Hikers hate its tangle of branches, but Hawaiians found many uses for this coastal species of hibiscus, with its buoyant, pliable wood and fibrous bark.

We shook the slender papaya trees, dislodging only the ripest fruit. Guavas were more plentiful, and the yellow lemon shapes littered the ground. Some had pinholes, which indicate that fruit fly maggots are inside. Some tasted sour.

"Look in the tree," said Chino. "If the birds have been feeding there, it's a sure sign the fruit is sweet."

At Ginger Pool, a white-rumped shama thrush was trilling sweetly as it hopped along a branch, adding its voice to the woodland music of water rushing over a stony streambed and the wind in the trees.

Farther up the valley, at Big Pool, mist drifted down from the plateau above, touching the eroded pinnacles with mystery. From time to time, sunbeams broke through the clouds, and the pinnacles emerged from the haze in a glow of light, like dreams remembered.

Anshu Reiskin, a former fashion coordinator from New York City, spent the night of September 10, 1992, at Big Pool, so she did not hear the wail of civil defense sirens at 5:30 the next morning. They were warning of a powerful hurricane bearing down on the island. It was called Iniki, which means "piercing winds." When it began to rain, Anshu decided to return to her tent on the beach.

In the meantime, one of the helicopter tour companies had evacuated all the campers it could find. By the time Anshu returned to the beach, it was deserted, and it was raining very hard.

"It was so weird. Kayaks, tents, and gear were everywhere, but there was no one around. I had no idea what was going on, but I thought I could wait out the storm in a cave. By that time the heavy rain had become torrential and thick with sand. It looked like a blizzard," she recalled.

Boulders started rolling off the cliffs. The gray ocean was lathered with foam. The plunge pool at the waterfall near the campgrounds had swollen into a lake that was spreading toward the cave.

"I knew I had to get out of there."

When she stepped out of the cave, the wind literally blew her down the beach. Winds were clocked at sustained speeds of more than 138 miles an hour, and gusts were gauged at about 180. A vortex wind spun her around and she fell, injuring her knee. She managed to crawl over to a cliff where winds pinned her against the wall. Thirty-foot waves exploded into raging surf that surged higher and higher up the beach. Rocks clattered down the cliffs. Branches flew through the air.

"I felt I was going to die. Then a frog jumped beside me. That contact with another living being gave me strength and determination to live. Somehow I crawled along the beach, praying the flying debris wouldn't hit me. The brief calm as the eye of the hurricane passed overhead gave me a break so I could make it up to the campground."

Demon winds had ripped dozens of trees out of the ground, and Anshu struggled to find her way through the havoc to the park's maintenance shack. Before long the winds returned and ripped the roof from its posts. Finally she found shelter in a small cave in back of the campground.

After a five-hour rampage, the storm passed, and that night a full moon shone in a starry sky.

Next morning the ocean was still white and foaming, washing tents and packs back onto shore. Branches and boulders littered the beach. Battered trees filled the air with the smell of fresh-cut wood. Amid the devastation, the cardinals and shama thrushes sang their morning songs, reestablishing the rhythm of a normal Kalalau day.

Anshu and four other survivors lived for three days on bananas and guavas until a U. S. Army medevac helicopter landed at Kalalau.

Much of the island had been ravaged by Iniki. The brutal winds demolished 2,000 homes, damaged 18,000 more, and toppled 5,000 utility poles, knocking out power and telephone lines. Pump stations carrying water to the island's subdivisions had been destroyed.

"Not one person was spared the wrath of Iniki," one island resident told me. Violent winds also delivered a heavy blow to the forests in its path. An aerial survey by the Division of Forestry and Wildlife reported that the vegetation in some areas looked like it had been "mowed by a giant weed-eater." Some of the valleys along the Na Pali coast funneled the winds into mini-tornadoes that flattened venerable old trees.

The hardest hit forests were completely leveled. Some trees remained upright but were so wind-blasted they lost their bark and soon died. Most trees that were merely stripped of their foliage survived and soon sprouted new growth that restored the island's lush look.

No one yet knows the final cost to the natural ecosystem.

"Normally after a hurricane like this, a native forest would recover in 50 or 100 years, but it's different now," says Steve Perlman. "Weeds in the ground are not going to give the native plants much chance. With the canopy gone, seeds that had been stymied by shade now have the benefit of sunlight and can accelerate their advance into the disturbed areas."

Despite the force of the hurricane, the rare plants Steve has been watching over have survived. Only their numbers are even fewer. Fortunately, the Alaka'i and its birds were largely spared.

Despite the ecological havoc on Kauai, Hawaii retains something of its unique natural heritage.

And despite the massacre of species that began when mankind found its way to these islands, it may not be too late to salvage this legacy. People are beginning to realize the special value of what was created in Hawaii. They have begun to care, and with that there is hope.

In a fitting climax to my visit, I accompanied a group of Hawaiians to Nu'alolo Kai, one of the valleys beyond Kalalau that is accessible only by boat. Here were sacred precincts, sanctified by ancient Hawaiian burials. Many Hawaiians attach great importance to bones, for it is believed they retain the person's *mana,* or spirit and power. In ancient times, bones were hidden so enemies could not use this mana. The one who interred the bones of a chief sometimes cut off his own tongue, so he could not reveal where they were hidden.

Members of the Hawaiian Burial Council came to the valley and in a solemn ceremony placed the bones that had been removed decades earlier by archaeologists in their original resting place.

"By returning the bones we make a statement that we care about the past and that we take pride in being Hawaiian," a friend explained. "If we can preserve our sense of our past and the uniqueness of our islands, the rest will come, for the fate of our treasures rests in human hands."

Hurricane Iniki scores a direct hit on Kauai in September 1992, with winds gusting to 180 mph. At Kōke'e State Park on the northwestern side of the island, trees and a cabin nearly vanish in a maelstrom of wind and rain.

DAVID BOYNTON

DAVID DOUBILET

Clutching a statue of the Virgin, a bewildered child at the town of Kekaha surveys her church and school, destroyed by Iniki's fury. Hawaii's worst storm in a century ripped off roofs and flattened homes at Lihue (above), the county seat. Rebuilding continues. Less easily repaired may be environmental upheaval: "In spots, the lush rain forest looked as though a giant weed whacker had rushed through," noted one observer. Scientists fear damage to native vegetation may accelerate gains by alien species.

Like gothic spires, cliffs of Kauai's Na Pali coast reach to the clouds. Once inhabitants farmed irrigated terraces in these remote, now uninhabited valleys. Today the spectacular coast draws hikers to its precipitous trails. Beckoning footsteps (below) invite beachcombing along Hanalei Bay.

FOLLOWING PAGES: Framed by lava sculptured over the ages, azure waters lap an idyllic strand at Honopū, accessible only by sea along Kauai's north coast.

DAVID BOYNTON

FRANS LANTING / MINDEN PICTURES (OPPOSITE); DOUGLAS PEEBLES (ABOVE)

MICHAEL S. YAMASHITA

"I was drawn to Hawaii by its picture-perfect beaches," says staff writer Cynthia Russ Ramsay. "But I soon discovered that its forests, deserts, and high country, with their unique array of plants and animals, are Hawaii's real treasures, along with the wonderful mix of people." Other assignments have taken Cynthia from Antarctica to Timbuktu.

ELIZABETH JOHNS

Chris Johns is a native of the Pacific Northwest now living in the Blue Ridge Mountains. In 1979, as a photographer at the Topeka Capital-Journal, *he was named Newspaper Photographer of the Year and also photographed his first National Geographic assignment. His* Valley of Life: Africa's Great Rift Valley *was published by Thomasson-Grant in 1992.*

ACKNOWLEDGMENTS

The Book Division wishes to thank the individuals, groups, and organizations named or quoted in the text for their assistance. We are especially grateful to Steven Lee Montgomery of the Bishop Museum, and to the superintendents and staff of Hawaii's parks and preserves. We would also like to thank George H. Balazs and William Gilmartin, National Marine Fisheries Service; Lance Bookless and Peter Schuyler, Division of Forestry and Wildlife; Brian Burnett, Office of State Planning; Leonard A. Freed and Robert A. Kinzie III, Dept. of Zoology, University of Hawaii; Lorin T. Gill, Moanalua Gardens; Paul Haraguchi, Hawaii Division of Water and Land Development; Carol Hopper, Waikiki Aquarium; Greg Kaufman, Pacific Whale Foundation; Jerry Leinecke, U. S. Fish and Wildlife Service; Maria Naehu, the Nature Conservancy; Ronald J. Nagata, Haleakala National Park; Storrs Olson, Museum of Natural History, Smithsonian Institution; Edwin Q. P. Petteys, Dept. of Land and Natural Resources, Lihue; Rita Pregana, Dan Taylor, and Frank Trusdell, Hawaii Volcanoes National Park; John E. Randall, the Bishop Museum; Marc Smith, Dept. of Land and Natural Resources, Hilo; Lani Stemmerman, University of Hawaii, Hilo; Raymond S. Tabata, Sea Grant Extension Service; Peter Thompson, Kalaupapa National Historical Park; and Joan Aidem, Sol Kahoohalahala, Sabra Kauka McCracken, and Pilipo Solatorio.

ADDITIONAL READING

Readers may wish to consult the *National Geographic Index* for related articles and books, as well as the following: John L. Culliney, *Islands in a Far Sea: Nature and Man in Hawaii;* Gavan Daws, *Islands of Life* and *Shoal of Time: A History of the Hawaiian Islands;* Ann Fielding and Ed Robinson, *An Underwater Guide to Hawaii;* Gregory Dean Kaufman and Paul Henry Forestell, *Hawaii's Humpback Whales;* Robert Louis Stevenson, *Travels in Hawaii;* Thomas L. Wright, et al., *Hawaii Volcano Watch: A Pictorial History, 1779-1991.*

Hawaii's Parks and Preserves

Several agencies in Hawaii administer numerous parks, reserves, and refuges, both for recreation and to protect rare individual species and ecosystems. Below are listed a few outstanding examples.

National Parks

◆ **HAWAII VOLCANOES:** For pyrotechnics Hawaii Volcanoes excels. Headquarters are perched 4,000 feet up on the rim of Kilauea, the world's most active volcano. The biggest land reserve by far in the state, with 229,177 acres, the park on the Big Island also takes in portions of vast Mauna Loa, largest volcano in the world.—*Hawaii 96718. Phone 808-967-7311.*

◆ **HALEAKALA:** This 28,655-acre park on Maui covers the eastern flank of Haleakala, from sea to summit. Legend portrays the demigod Maui capturing the sun here. A spectacularly steep drive climbs fog-collared slopes to the sun-crowned, 10,000-foot summit. Attractions include cinder cones, where unusual endemic silverswords and nene geese live, and a visit to coastal Kīpahulu.—*P.O. Box 369, Makawao, Maui, Hawaii 96768. Phone 808-572-9306.*

National Historical Parks

◆ **KALAUPAPA:** This site encompasses a leprosy settlement occupying a serenely beautiful peninsula on Molokai's isolated north coast. A few victims of Hansen's disease still live here, but by choice.—*Kalaupapa, Hawaii 96742. Phone 808-567-6102.*

◆ **PU'UHONUA O HONAUNAU:** On the Big Island, this was once a place of refuge, where lawbreakers found sanctuary. Its temples, images, and stone walls have been carefully restored.—*P.O. Box 129, Honaunau, Kona, Hawaii 96726. Phone 808-328-2326.*

◆ **KALOKO-HONOKOHAU:** Newly opened to the public, this park contains numerous archaeological sites, including the Mamalahoa Trail, or King's Highway, which once encircled the entire island of Hawaii.—*73-4786 Kanalani Street, #14, Kailua-Kona, Hawaii 96740. Phone 808-329-6881.*

State Parks

An extensive system includes some 65 units that vary from small waysides and recreational beaches to historical enclaves and wilderness retreats.

On Hawaii

◆ **'AKAKA FALLS:** An easy stroll brings visitors to the 442-foot falls, as well as to 100-foot Kahuna Falls.

◆ **KEALAKEKUA BAY:** Underwater park provides snorkeling and scuba diving in coral reefs and other marine habitats.—*Dept. of Land and Natural Resources, Division of State Parks, P.O. Box 936, Hilo, Hawaii 96721-0936. Phone 808-933-4200.*

On Kauai

◆ **KOKE'E:** This 4,345-acre park offers access to Alaka'i Swamp and other forest reserves.

◆ **WAIMEA CANYON:** Spectacular 14-mile-long gorge cuts more than 3,000 feet into the Kōke'e Plateau.

◆ **NA PALI COAST:** The rugged 11-mile Kalalau Trail leads hikers through remote valleys along Kauai's north coast.—*For camping permit: Dept. of Land and Natural Resources, Division of State Parks, 3060 Eiwa Street, Lihue, Hawaii 96766-1875. Phone 808-241-3444.*

On Oahu

◆ **KAHANA VALLEY:** 5,220-acre beach-to-mountaintop park offers hiking, camping, and Hawaiian cultural programs for scheduled groups.—*Dept. of Land and Natural Resources, Division of State Parks, P.O. Box 621, Honolulu, Hawaii 96809. Phone 808-587-0300.*

National Wildlife Refuges

The refuges encompass nine preserves that range from **PEARL HARBOR**, wetlands on densely populated Oahu, and the **HAKALAU FOREST**, rain forest on the Big Island, to far-flung **HAWAIIAN ISLANDS**, which embraces remote islands and atolls. Only **KILAUEA POINT**, on Kauai's north coast, offers public access for observation of passing monk seals, green turtles, great frigate birds, and red-footed boobies.—*For information on Kilauea: P.O. Box 87, Kilauea, Kauai, Hawaii 96754. Phone 808-541-1201. Permission required for others. Contact: Complex Project Leader, Hawaiian and Pacific Islands NWRs, U. S. Fish and Wildlife Service, 300 Ala Moana Blvd., P.O. Box 50167, Honolulu, Hawaii 96850. Phone 808-541-1201.*

Natural Area Reserves and Forest Reserves

The 50 forest reserves cover 1.2 million acres, more than 30 percent of Hawaii's land area. The reserves assure the population of the islands a reliable water supply by protecting springs, streams, and watershed areas on the islands.

The 19 natural area reserves, often located adjacent to other parks and reserves, occupy more than 100,000 acres and protect a variety of habitats and natural resources. Write or phone for permits.—*Natural Area Reserves System / Forest Reserves, Dept. of Land and Natural Resources, 1151 Punchbowl Street, Honolulu, Hawaii 96813. Natural Areas phone 808-587-0063. Forest Reserves phone 808-587-0166.*

Nature Conservancy

The Nature Conservancy, with numerous holdings, helps preserve and restore Hawaii's natural heritage.

◆ **WAIKAMOI PRESERVE:** Easily accessible from Haleakala, this 5,320-acre preserve contains high elevation tropical rain forest, habitat for 12 Hawaiian bird species, and hundreds of plants and animals that exist nowhere else. Hikes are regularly scheduled.—*Preserve Manager, P.O. Box 1716, Makawao, Maui, Hawaii 96768. Phone 808-572-7849.*

Index

Boldface indicates illustrations.

Library of Congress CIP data

Ramsay, Cynthia Russ.

Hawaii's hidden treasures / by Cynthia Russ Ramsay ; photographed by Chris Johns ; prepared by the Book Division, National Geographic Society, Washington, D. C.
p. cm.
Includes index.
ISBN 0-87044-909-5
1. Natural History—Hawaii. 2. Nature conservation—Hawaii. I. Johns, Chris. II. National Geographic Society (U.S.). Book Division. III. Title.
QH198.H3R36 1993
508.969—dc20
93-6307
CIP

Composition for this book by the National Geographic Society Book Division with the assistance of the Typographic section of National Geographic Production Services, Pre-Press Division. Set in ITC New Baskerville. Printed and bound by R. R. Donnelley & Sons, Willard, Ohio. Color separations by Graphic Art Service, Inc., Nashville, Tenn.; Lanman Progressive Co., Washington, D.C.; Lincoln Graphics, Inc., Cherry Hill, N.J.; and Phototype Color Graphics, Pennsauken, N.J. Dust jacket printed by Miken Systems, Inc., Cheektowaga, N.Y.